ABILITY

Landmark Judgments on
Disability Jurisprudence in India

ABILITY

Landmark Judgments on Disability Jurisprudence in India

Navdeep Singh

Shruti Bedi

THE BROWSER

Title: Ability: Landmark Judgments on
Disability Jurisprudence in India
Editors: Navdeep Singh and Shruti Bedi

ISBN: 978-93-49042-37-7

Published by:
JGS Enterprises Pvt Ltd
Imprint: The Browser

Publisher's Address:
SCO 14-15, FF, Sector 8-C, Chandigarh 160 009

Website: thebrowser.org
Email: service@thebrowser.org

© Layout and Cover Design by beagles
99beagles.com

Contents

Foreword by Justice Surya Kant .... *vii*

About the Editors .... *ix*

Introduction .... *xi*

1. Transformative Equality for Disabled Persons: *Ravinder Kumar Dhariwal v. Union of India*
   Justice A.K. Sikri 1

2. Justice through a New Lens: *In Re: Recruitment of Visually Impaired in Judicial Services v. The Registrar General, High Court of Madhya Pradesh*
   Justice Rekha Palli 16

3. The Conundrum over the Guardianship of Comatose Patients: *Shobha Gopalakrishnan v. State of Kerala*
   Justice Rajive Bhalla 29

4. Streamlining the Admission Process to Medical Institutions for the Disabled: *Omkar Ramchandra Gond v. Union of India*
   Prof. Balram K. Gupta 41

5. Disability Discrimination at the Workplace – A Case for Compassion: *Bhagwan Dass v. Punjab State Electricity Board*
   Francisca Pretorius 58

6. Inaugurating a Discourse of Autonomy and Choice: *Suchita Srivastava v. Chandigarh Administration*
Prof. Amita Dhanda 71

7. A Supreme Court Ruling that Gave Wings to the Disabled: *Jeeja Ghosh v. Union of India*
Manraj Grewal Sharma 85

8. Disability and Cinema – Addressing Negative Stereotypes and Shifting Narratives: *Nipun Malhotra v. Sony Pictures Films India Private Limited*
Sanjeev Sharma & Kritika Sharma 96

9. The Suffering Beneath the Tough Façade – Disabilities in the Military: *Ashish Kumar Chauhan v. Commanding Officer*
Arjun Sheoran & Major D.P. Singh...114

10. Do Persons with Disabilities Have the Right to Reservation in Promotion?: *State of Kerala v. Leesamma Joseph*
Raj Kumar Makkad & Himani Makkad...129

11. The Right to Education from the Child's Perspective, a Mirage? An Existential Grey Zone?: *Rajneesh Kumar Pandey v. Union of India*
Shabnam Aggarwal...143

12. A Glimmer of Hope: *Vikash Kumar v. Union Public Service Commission*
Srianusha Thotakura & Apoorva Pushkarna 158

13. Uncovering and Dislodging the Constructedness of Structural Ableism: *Disabled Rights Group v. Union of India*
Jaideep Singh Lalli & Ananya Sharma...172

Surya Kant
Judge, Supreme Court of India

19, Akbar Road,
New Delhi-110011.

Phone : 011-23793060
E-mail : pstojusticesuryakant@gmail.com

FOREWORD

There are certain sensitive topics within the realm of law, that need a delicate approach. Disability jurisprudence is one of them. It is a theme that not just involves law in its classical sense but also places emotion, compassion, empathy, and a constructive interpretation of the written word into meaningful practice.

I am glad Navdeep and Shruti have been able to collect, edit and curate these eloquent essays into one compelling compilation which makes for an easy reading even for a layperson not connected with the legal profession. Each essay deals with a separate judgment, and though there might be inter-sectional learnings, every piece presents a different perspective, reflecting to an extent, the point of view of the author. The judgments discussed in this volume represent not just legal precedents but also powerful narratives that challenge discrimination, advocate for inclusion, and affirm the rights of individuals with disabilities. They echo the ongoing struggle for recognition and equality in a world that too often marginalizes those who do not fit the conventional mould.

What makes it more readable is the fact that the essays have been written by personalities from varied fields - from seasoned judges and lawyers to academicians, journalists, young professionals, and specially abled persons themselves, giving each chapter a refreshing feel rather than being encumbered with an indistinctive essence. This volume is a testament to the collective efforts of those who strive for a more equitable society, one where the rights of individuals with disabilities are not just recognized but celebrated.

While there can be no two ways about the fact that as a society we must move towards more progressive practices in this field with expectation of robust support from all stakeholders, publications like these provide a guiding light with practical experiences on how to walk that talk. Institutional support to this subject is also a must. We must play our small little roles to make that happen, and the recent contribution of the Supreme Court of India in releasing the "Handbook Concerning Persons with Disabilities" was one such step towards this avowed aim.

I congratulate the editors, authors, and the publishers for making this book a reality, and sincerely hope that it would prove to be a sturdy and long-lasting contribution to this field.

[Justice Surya Kant]
07-05-2025

About the Editors

Navdeep Singh

A practicing lawyer at the Punjab & Haryana High Court, India on the constitutional side, Major Navdeep Singh is a practitioner of constitutional law and a globally recognised expert of military-related law and reform in administration of justice, including military justice. He has also worked in the fields of disability and gender rights jurisprudence. He was the founder President of the Armed Forces Tribunal Bar Association, Chandigarh, India and is a decorated former Territorial Army reservist-volunteer. He was a Member-Participant at the drafting of the "Yale Draft" at the *Yale Law School* and was also on the drafting committee of the "Commonwealth Military Justice Principles" (The "Stellenbosch Draft").

He is a former Member of a high-level Committee of Experts constituted by the Indian Ministry of Defence on directions of the Prime Minister to reduce litigation and initiate reform in redressal of grievances in the Armed Forces. He is Member of *International Society for Military Law and the Law of War* at Brussels, the first International Fellow of the *National Institute of Military Justice* at Washington DC, and one of the five appointed members of the military justice advisory committee of the *Commonwealth Secretariat*, London. Major Singh has authored and edited multiple books, articles and opinion pieces on law, public policy and military topics and has also spoken at various national and international universities and institutions of repute. His last co-edited book was *In Her Defence: Ten Landmark Judgments on Women in the Armed Forces* (Penguin, 2024). He is also one of the Honorary Chief Editors of the *Forces Law Review*, the world's first global military law journal

Professor Shruti Bedi

A distinguished Professor of Law and Director at the University Institute of Legal Studies, Panjab University, Chandigarh, Professor (Dr.) Shruti Bedi is an expert in constitutional law, heads the *Centre for Constitution and Public Policy*, Panjab University and also serves as Honorary Chief Editor of *Forces Law Review*, the world's first global military law journal. She is an International Fellow at the *National Institute of Military Justice*, Washington DC, and Visiting Professor at Universitas Airlangga, Indonesia.

Recognised for her contributions to legal thought and public service, Prof. Bedi is a TEDx speaker and recipient of *The Phenomenal She* Award (2022) conferred by the Indian National Bar Association. She has also been honoured by the British Deputy High Commission for her role in strengthening Indo-UK collaboration.

Her academic work spans constitutional law, counterterrorism, and the regulation of emerging technologies, particularly artificial intelligence. With over eleven authored and edited volumes and more than 90 scholarly publications, her notable works include *Shaping the Judges: Essays in Honour of Dr. Balram K. Gupta* (Law & Justice, 2025), *Indian Counter Terrorism Law* (LexisNexis, 2016), *Judicial Review: Process, Powers and Problems* (Cambridge University Press, 2020), and *Artificial Intelligence and Constitutionalism* (Oakbridge, 2024). Prof Bedi has delivered lectures and engaged in academic collaborations with leading institutions across the globe including the University of Toronto, University of Ottawa, Nottingham Trent University, Pontifical Catholic University of Paraná (Brazil), and Vietnam National University.

Introduction

The Supreme Court of India, the court of last resort for the oppressed, is often referred to as the 'People's Court'. In the mind of the marginalised individual, it occupies a hallowed place as it is seen as the ultimate protector of their rights. Today, as one in seven persons in the world lives with a disability, it is time to assess the discrimination faced by Persons with Disabilities (PwD) with a remedial and rights-based lens. The entrenched stigma and ostracism towards PwD are widespread, often compounding the barriers they already face in accessing education, employment, healthcare, and public spaces. India's legislative journey in this realm began with *the Persons with Disabilities (Equal Opportunities, Protection of Rights and Full Participation) Act, 1995*, and was given renewed momentum through the more progressive *Rights of Persons with Disabilities Act, 2016.* Yet, beyond statutory text, it is the judiciary that has played a transformative role—infusing spirit into the letter of the law, interpreting it dynamically, and crafting a more inclusive vision of justice.

This book is an anthology of thirteen landmark judgments delivered by constitutional courts in India on the issue of disability jurisprudence. It seeks to position these judgments as powerful commentaries on the rights of the disabled, both within and beyond the courtroom. The dichotomy between the disabled and non-disabled is not always intentional, but arises from systemic exclusion and the lived realities of those at the margins. The title of this book—*Ability*—is both a provocation and an assertion. It signals a shift from viewing disability through a lens of incapacity to one of potential, resilience, and rightful inclusion. The book aims to present these judgments as sites of transformation, not just in law, but in the social and institutional frameworks that govern our lives.

The Supreme Court's ruling in *Vikash Kumar v. Union Public Service Commission* (2021) marks a pivotal moment, where the principle of *reasonable accommodation* was explicitly anchored into Indian jurisprudence, drawing from the UNCRPD and affirming substantive equality. In *Ravinder Dhariwal v. Union of India* (2021), Article 14 was expansively interpreted to include the obligation of inclusive equality and equitable treatment for persons with disabilities, particularly in public employment. Similarly, *Suchita Srivastava v. Chandigarh Administration* (2009) remains a foundational case recognising the reproductive autonomy of intellectually disabled women, situating their rights under Article 21 of the Constitution.

In *Ashish Kumar Chauhan v. Union of India* (2023), the Court held the defence services vicariously liable for medical negligence during military service, resulting in the contraction of HIV through a transfusion—marking a rare instance where compensation and accountability were awarded within a strict institutional context. The Court further expressed the need for systemic attitudinal reform in how disabled military personnel are perceived and treated. In *Bhagwan Dass v. Punjab State Electricity Board* (2008), the wrongful termination of a disabled employee led to a landmark reinstatement order, reinforcing employment protections under the disability rights framework.

In *Rajneesh Kumar Pandey v. Union of India* (2021), the Court issued detailed directions to ensure inclusive education for children with special needs in mainstream institutions. The scope of reservation was further expanded in *Leesamma Joseph v. State of Kerala* (2021), where the Supreme Court confirmed the right of PwD to promotions under Article 16(4), affirming that the principle of equality must percolate into career progression and leadership roles. In *Disabled Rights Group v. Union of India* (2018), the apex court ruled on wide-ranging issues including reservation of seats in higher education and ensuring accessibility in public and private spaces, calling for active compliance by institutions.

The Kerala High Court in *Shobha Gopalakrishnan v. State of Kerala* (2019) addressed a critical legislative vacuum by formulating guidelines for the appointment of guardians for patients in a comatose state, empowering families to manage essential legal and financial affairs. In *Jeeja Ghosh v. Union of India* (2016), the Supreme Court came down strongly on discriminatory airline practices, recognising the dignity of a woman with cerebral palsy who was deboarded unceremoniously from a flight—an important step in embedding sensitivity and inclusion in the travel sector.

The issue of accessibility within the judiciary itself came into sharp focus in *In Re: Recruitment of Visually Impaired in Judicial Services v. The Registrar General, High Court of Madhya Pradesh* (2025), where the Court addressed the systemic exclusion of visually impaired candidates from judicial services, asserting that access to the judiciary must extend not only to litigants but also to those who aspire to serve on the bench. In *Omkar Ramchandra Gond v. Union of India* (2024), the Supreme Court intervened to ensure that disabled candidates were not unfairly excluded from medical admissions, directing institutions to frame equitable procedures that respected the capabilities and rights of all aspirants. In *Nipun Malhotra v. Sony Pictures Films India Pvt. Ltd.* (2024), the Court addressed the harmful portrayal of disability in mainstream cinema, emphasising the duty of content creators to uphold the constitutional principles of dignity and non-discrimination.

In the vast tapestry of human rights, the rights of PwD are often woven into the broader social fabric without being distinctly acknowledged. This book aims to place them at the forefront by illuminating the far-reaching consequences of these judicial decisions. While civil society has played a formidable role in advocating for these rights, with official efforts such as the *Pathways to Access* handbook issued by the Department of Empowerment of Persons with Disabilities (Ministry of Social Justice & Empowerment, Government of India), true transformation requires continued vigilance, implementation, and awareness.

Crafted by a diverse and distinguished collective of judges, legal scholars, activists, educators, and commentators, this anthology makes complex legal ideas accessible to the general reader. Each chapter distils the essence of a landmark ruling, unpacking both its legal reasoning and the socio-emotional realities it addresses. The objective is not only to inform but also to initiate a larger dialogue on dignity, justice, and inclusion.

By bringing together judicial reasoning and lived experience, this book underscores that the story of disability law is also a story of resistance, resilience, and reform. These thirteen cases represent more than isolated legal victories—they map the changing landscape of India's legal and moral imagination. As readers engage with these stories, we hope they will be moved not only to understand but to act—to challenge perceptions, confront prejudice, and uphold the constitutional promise of equality for all.

We gratefully acknowledge the unstinting support of our publisher. A special word of thanks to Ananya Sharma for her thoughtful assistance.

Navdeep Singh Shruti Bedi

Transformative Equality for Disabled Persons

Ravinder Kumar Dhariwal v. Union of India

Justice A.K. Sikri

The two important and profound messages we get from Chapter IV of the Constitution of India relating to 'Fundamental Rights' are equality and dignity. The principle of equality warrants that everyone should be treated equally irrespective of caste, creed, religion, sex, etc. Though dignity is not specifically mentioned in this Chapter, the flavour of the entire Chapter is based on dignity. In fact, dignity is the fulcrum of human rights. The rights of persons suffering from disabilities, physical or mental, or otherwise, are to be investigated from this prism.

The word 'disability' is an amalgam of two words – 'dis' and 'ability'. There is an inherent negative connotation prefixed to it. This results in a negative implication, which is often derived when we refer to a handicapped individual. This further entrenches one's feeling of being disabled. To do away with the traditional approach, a more inclusive term – differently abled – was used to describe this group of people. The idea behind the use of the term was to pull focus from their limitations towards what they can do. However, it is also important to state that 'Persons with Disabilities' is now considered the most appropriate term.

We often forget that disability is not by choice, but by chance. Similarly, such persons do not suffer as much from 'disability' as they do from 'discrimination'. As per the guidelines issued by the UN Disability Inclusion Strategy, they suggest the usage of People-first language. Like how our 1995 Act is coined – 'The Persons with Disability'. Viewing disability through a charitable lens perpetuates stereotypes and reinforces systemic inequalities. Instead, society should focus on dismantling barriers and creating inclusive environments where individuals with disabilities can thrive autonomously.

The harsh reality, as encountered by this class, is altogether different. In the book on the rights of disabled persons authored by Joseph P. Shapiro, which is titled *No Pity*,[1] the first chapter, 'Introduction' has the sub-title 'You Just Don't Understand' and the very first sentence of the said book is: 'Non-disabled Americans do not understand disabled ones.'

We may modify the aforesaid statement by substituting the word 'Americans' with 'persons' as the aforesaid statement is not limited to Americans alone, but is applicable across the universe. Though there is a marked improvement in the perception of society about disabled persons, things are moving at a slow pace. No doubt, we have come a long way from the days when persons with disability faced not only discrimination but even non-inclusivity in society. From that stage, the world moved to the next level when the approach towards disabled persons came to be seen as a health and welfare issue, to be addressed through care provided to them from a charitable point of view. At this level, the disabled persons are viewed as abnormal, deserving of pity and care, and not as individuals who are entitled

1. Joseph P. Shapiro, *No Pity: People with Disabilities Forging a New Civil Rights Movement* (Indian reprint by Universal Book Traders, New Delhi, 1993)

to enjoy the same opportunities to live a full and satisfying life as other members of society. This resulted in marginalising the disabled persons and their exclusion both from the mainstream of society and the enjoyment of their fundamental rights and freedoms. Disability tends to be couched within a medical and welfare framework, identifying Persons with Disabilities as ill, different from their non-disabled peers, and in need of care. Because the emphasis is on the medical needs of Persons with Disabilities, there is a corresponding neglect of their wider social needs, which has resulted in severe isolation for Persons with Disabilities and their families.

However, nations moved forward from that stage as well, at least on paper. Real awareness has dawned on society at large that the problems of the disabled are to be viewed from a human rights perspective. This thinking is reflected in two major declarations on disability adopted by the General Assembly of the United Nations on 20 December 1971 and subsequently in 1975 and in order to convert the resolutions adopted therein into reality, the Indian Parliament also passed the enactment i.e., Persons with Disabilities (Equal Opportunities, Protection of Rights and Full Participation) Act, 1995, which is substituted by another enactment in 2016 viz., Rights of Persons with Disabilities Act (RPwD Act) conferring the rights more liberally.

These rights conferred upon such persons have sent an eloquent message that there is no question of sympathising with such persons and extending them medical or other help. What is to be borne in mind is that they are also human beings and they must grow as normal persons and are to be extended all facilities in this regard. The subject of the rights of persons with disabilities should be approached from a human rights perspective, which recognises that persons with disabilities are entitled to enjoy the full range of internationally guaranteed rights and freedoms without discrimination on the ground of disability.

Though the law now recognises and has granted various rights to disabled persons to ensure their inclusivity in society and to provide them with all necessary facilities to overcome their disabilities and become an important part of society, the struggle to enjoy these rights is far from over. It becomes the duty of the State to take positive measures to enable this class of persons to exercise these rights. This, in turn, casts a heavy burden on the judiciary, apart from the executive, to enforce these rights by creating conducive jurisprudence with a purposive interpretation of the statutory provisions.

It is vehemently argued that the Constitution is silent as to the rights of the disabled, but on a purposive interpretation of the Fundamental Rights, these rights are available to all persons. That is the message of many landmark pronouncements of the judiciary.

When society fails to eradicate this discrimination against one set of people, the judiciary must take charge. The Australian Human Rights Commission coined a term in its 1992 Act,[2] which explains that disability discrimination occurs when a person is treated less favourably, or not given the same opportunities as others in a similar situation, because of their disability.

The Indian Supreme Court has protected the rights of the disabled under the blanket of Articles 14 and 21 of the Constitution of India. The right to life given under Article 21 purposely interprets and includes disabled persons while stating that the right to life means life with dignity and not just mere animal existence. The Supreme Court, so far, through its judgments, has established two fundamental principles: that persons with impairment/disability are rights-holders and that disability manifests only when it prevents such individuals from doing the tasks that they desire.

2. Australian Government, 'Disability Discrimination Act, 1992', available at: https://www.legislation.gov.au/C2004A04426/2018-04-12/text (accessed 24 August 2024)

Various landmark judgments have been pronounced by the apex court (and even by various High Courts), thereby making the judiciary a catalyst for reforms. One recent pronouncement in the category of profound and distinguished judgment is *Ravinder Kumar Dhariwal and Another v. Union of India and Others.*[3] Analysis of this judgment will bring about its sterling nature.

Case of *Ravinder Kumar Dhariwal*

The brief factual matrix of the case is that the Appellant had joined the Central Reserve Police Force (CRPF) in November 2001. During the tenure of his service, the Deputy Inspector General (DIG) of Police lodged a complaint against the Appellant, alleging his unstable mental condition. The complaint noted that the DIG suspected that the Appellant was obsessed with either killing or being killed and made a threat that he could shoot. Subsequently, an enquiry was held against the Appellant under Rule 14 of Central Civil Services (CCS) (Classification, Control, and Appeal) Rules 1965, and six points of charges were framed against the Appellant. Following the complaint, the Appellant was suspended. A second enquiry was conducted, wherein he was held liable for leaving the headquarters without depositing his pistol and ammunition. A Standing Order had been passed by the Department earlier, constituting a Rehabilitation Board, subjecting individuals to critical examination to determine their fitness for rehabilitation. However, subsequently, this order was altered. The Appellant was awarded the punishment of withholding two increments in his pay scale. A third enquiry was initiated against the Appellant on the charge that he was absent without permission while he was under suspension. Meanwhile, the Appellant was declared permanently disabled by two different hospitals, having 40 to 70 percent

3. (2023) 2 SCC 209

disability. The medical report stated that the Appellant was unfit for duty, and the report placed him under the S5(P) category (low medical category) due to his partial and limited response to all modalities of treatment since 2009.

The Appellant challenged the above first enquiry report in a Writ Petition (WP) before the High Court. While relying on the law laid down in *Kunal Singh v. Union of India* [4] and the mandatory nature of Section 47 of the Persons with Disabilities (PwD) (Equal Opportunities, Protection of Rights and Full Participation) Act, 1995 (hereinafter '1995 Act'), the court held that since the Appellant had acquired the disability during the course of his service, the Respondents were bound to consider the case of the Appellant vis- à-vis the mandatory provisions under Section 47 of the 1995 Act.

The Respondents, being aggrieved, appealed to the Division Bench. They contended that the Appellant had not referred to having suffered from disability (Obsessive-Compulsive Disorder or OCD) in his reply to the enquiry against him and had only raised the issue for the first time in the writ petition. Agreeing with the Respondents, the Bench restored the enquiry proceedings against the Appellant to the stage of recording of evidence, and the Appellant was allowed to plead the defence of his mental condition in reply to the enquiry and the article of charges levelled against him.

Aggrieved by the above order, the Appellant filed a Special Leave Petition before the Supreme Court.

Approach Taken by the Court

Three steps were taken by the court throughout its review of the case. Initially, the court elevated the concepts of 'dignity' and 'equality' under Section 3 to a background value, suggesting

4. (2003) 4 SCC 524

that they are a fundamental obligation of the Act. This measure recognised the State's positive obligation to guarantee the rights of individuals with disabilities, as outlined in the same provision. Secondly, it employed the Mental Healthcare Act, 2017,[5] as a supporting authority to underscore the State's intention to establish a framework for mental health rights.

Finally, the court employed international jurisprudence in elaborating the definition of 'non-discrimination in employment' under Section 20 of the Rights of Persons with Disabilities Act, 2016 which mandates that the State not discriminate against any person in matters pertaining to employment and provide reasonable accommodations to employees with disabilities, in order to counter and address the arguments of the Respondent, namely, that the aspect of mental disability was not raised prior to the proceedings in the Supreme Court and second, that the Appellant did not produce himself before the medical officer of the force for treatment. The court's decision improves the status of those who suffer from mental health disorders, but there is also a chance that the logic it employed to reach its third-step decision could serve as a benchmark for future judicial reviews.[6]

Reliance on International Jurisprudence

The court noted that mental disability rights in India are still in their infancy, which justified its use of foreign sources as compelling jurisprudence. However, the recent decision in *Lieutenant Colonel*

---

5. Mental Healthcare Act, 2017, Act No. 10 of 2017, available at: https://www.indiacode.nic.in/bitstream/123456789/2249/1/A2017-10.pdf

6. Arif Mustafa Hussain, 'Transformative Equality: The Supreme Court on Mental Disability and Anti-Discrimination', *NUALS Law Journal* (17 February 2022), available at: https://nualslawjournal.com/2022/02/17/transformative-equality-the-supreme-court-on-mental-disability-and-anti-discrimination/ (accessed 25 August 2024)

Nitisha v. Union of India,[7] where Justice Chandrachud J., as he then was, acknowledged and addressed indirect gender discrimination towards women officers of the Indian Army, is also responsible for the use of international jurisprudence in identifying indirect discrimination and invalidating discriminatory practices.

The court emphasised the need to identify the causal relationship between the practice or provision and the disproportionate impact it has on a person who is disadvantaged, as established by the UK Supreme Court in the *Essop v. Home Office*[8] (UK Border Agency) case. In addition, the court cited the *Ontario Human Rights Commission v. Simpsons-Sears*[9] decision, in which the Canadian Supreme Court held that imposing a restriction, even inadvertently, can be discriminatory. The Indian Supreme Court used this insight to change its position from one of formal equality, which emphasises treating everyone equally, to one of substantive equality, which considers the unique traits of the affected class.

Drawing inspiration from the previously cited case, the court in this particular issue first read through Article 12 of the Convention on the Rights of Persons with Disabilities,[10] specifically, Explanation 1.[11] This proved that there has been a change from the 'substitution' model, which requires a decision-maker to give consent on behalf of the disabled person, to the

7. (2021) 15 SCC 125

8. (2017) UKSC 27

9. (1985) 2 SCR 536

10. Convention on the Rights of Persons with Disabilities and Optional Protocol, available at: https://www.un.org/disabilities/documents/convention/convoptprot-e.pdf

11. 'General Comment No. 1 (2014) – Article 12: Equal Recognition before the Law' (Committee on the Rights of Persons with Disabilities), available at: https://digitallibrary.un.org/record/812024?v=pdf

'support' model,[12] which acknowledges their legal capacity and offers them an alternative setting in which to make decisions. This justification is significant because it provides a socio-legal foundation for requiring the use of reasonable accommodations. The court observed that:

> On a combined reading of the definitions provided in Section 2(s) and 2 (c) of the Act, it is evident that the RPwD – similar to the 2017 Act – defines disability as a social construct and not solely as a medical construct.[13]

Interestingly, the definition of 'disadvantageous' in the context of the relevant statutes was based on Article 12 of the Convention,[14] which served as the foundational standard for interpreting their contents. Although the statute clearly acknowledges the State's positive commitment to provide reasonable accommodations, there are no court precedents in India that address the firing of a mental health worker whose job involves following a code of conduct. As such, the court employed foreign jurisprudence to contextualise mental disability via the anti-discrimination lens, so striking a balance between the right to reasonable accommodation and workplace norms and expectations.

The first significant case was *Den Hartog v. Wasatch Academy*,[15] in which the United States Court of Appeals for the Tenth Circuit established the 'direct threat' standard, which prioritises the essential duties of the position and only permits reasonable accommodations for behaviours that are both tolerable and directly

12. *Supra* note 6

13. *Supra* note 3, para 70

14. *Supra* note 6

15. 129 F.3d 1076 (1997)

related to the disability. This test established the groundwork for a greater reliance on 'causal connection' in the event of a disability, even though it does not fully incorporate a rights-based approach.

The minority opinion in *Stewart v. Elk Valley Coal Corp.*,[16] a case determined by the Supreme Court of Canada involving the discharge of a coal mine worker who tested positive for drugs, then clarified the proper application of the reasonable accommodation responsibility. Although the majority opinion held that there was no discrimination because the drug policy test, which did not specifically target a protected group, was the reason for the dismissal rather than the addiction, Gascon J. noted that even a neutral policy that applies to all employees equally will fall under the category of indirect discrimination. This dissent was justified by the argument that a decision based on a policy formulated with the interests of the majority in mind would treat disabled people in the same way as able-bodied people. In essence, this would mean removing the protections granted to people with impairments. The establishment of an individualised evaluation system and acknowledging the employee's diminished agency as a result of their impairment were two additional critical components of the Supreme Court's minority ruling.

The Supreme Court of India in the instant case established that a dismissal based on a mental handicap would be deemed discriminatory, thereby establishing the principle of causal link under the anti-discrimination test. This was made possible by the combined reading of the two aforementioned rulings. In its ruling, the court noted that although it is standard procedure to initiate disciplinary actions against CRPF employees for misconduct, this procedure has put the Appellant at a 'disproportionate' disadvantage because he is more likely than other able-bodied employees to engage in behaviour that could be an indication of misconduct.

16. 2017 SCC 30

Formulation of a Standard for Judicial Review

The Supreme Court has held that this method is only the beginning and that it can only serve as inspiration within pre-existing judicial review standards because it does not provide a definitive interpretation of Section 20 of the Act.

> The jurisprudence of Sections 3 and 20 of the RPwD Act would have to evolve. Our journey has begun. Here we have pondered over the possible trappings which a standard of judicial review may adopt.[17]

Nonetheless, one may argue that the development of a discriminatory test can serve as a benchmark in determining the rights under the Act of individuals with mental disorders. One way to interpret the test is as follows: First, the worker needs to be in a disadvantageous situation. Second, any action that violates workplace policies should be considered an aversive action against the employee. To further compound the disadvantage, the disagreeable action should have a direct causal relationship to the employee's mental handicap. A violation of Section 20 of the Act would result from satisfying the aforementioned three requirements, which would nevertheless grant the affected person the right to reasonable accommodation.

Conclusion

This judgment is one of the finest examples of judicial craftsmanship and amply demonstrates how, with the aid of interpretative tools and human rights jurisprudence – domestic as well as international – the rights of disabled persons under the statutes can be fine-

17. *Supra* note 3, para 145

tuned, chiselled, and applied to advance the purpose behind these statutes. This is apparent from the fact that even when the court found that the instant case was governed by Section 47 of the PwD Act, by an innovative approach, the court applied the provisions of Section 20 of the RPwD Act holding that even if the PwD Act is held applicable when disciplinary proceedings were started, the privilege that the Respondent possessed under the 2002 notification issued under PwD Act exempting the CRPF from the operation of Section 47 of the said Act would be an abstract of inchoate privilege unless the privilege has been acted upon by the Respondent.

On that reckoning, the court proceeded to hold that even when the CRPF has the privilege to terminate, demote, or deny promotion to employees with disabilities, it does not have the privilege to discriminate against a disabled employee in any manner relating to employment. It went on to hold that if two interpretations are possible, then the interpretation that is in consonance with international law or gives effect to international law must be used. That apart, the court also held three facets of discrimination that guide the PwD Act:

1. Right to formal equality;
2. Affirmative action in pursuance of substantive equality under Section 33; and
3. Reasonable accommodation of persons as provided under Section 47.[18]

This judgment, therefore, stands apart on the horizon when it comes to the rights of Persons with Disabilities and gives a message to society in general and the judiciary in particular, 'where there is a will, there is a way'.

18. *Supra* note 3, para 40

While analysing the pattern in the way the courts deliver justice, it is often noticed that the judgments always prioritise the rights and needs of disabled individuals. This judicial approach is deeply rooted in the principles of equality, non-discrimination, and human dignity, which are enshrined in various national constitutions and international legal frameworks such as the United Nations Convention on the Rights of Persons with Disabilities (UNCRPD). Courts meticulously interpret and enforce laws to guarantee that disabled individuals receive fair treatment and have equal access to opportunities and resources. By doing so, the judiciary plays a crucial role in dismantling systemic barriers, empowering disabled individuals, and fostering an inclusive society where everyone can thrive and participate fully, irrespective of their physical or mental abilities. These decisions underscore the judiciary's role in promoting social integration for disabled persons.

We look forward to such judicial creativity that endeavours to make the lives of persons in this class more meaningful and productive.

Justice A.K. Sikri

Justice Arjan Kumar Sikri is presently an International Judge, Singapore International Commercial Court, and a former Judge, Supreme Court of India. He currently holds the following positions: Chairperson of the Committee for Formulating an Action Plan for Online Dispute Resolution under NITI Aayog, Government of India; Chairperson of the Oversight Committee and High Powered Committee of the Char Dham Project appointed by the Supreme Court of India; Member, Board of Directors of Mediators Beyond Borders International (MBBI) with headquarters in the US; Chairman of News Broadcasting & Digital Standards Authority (NBDSA); Chairperson, Grievance Redressal Board, Digital Publisher Content Grievances Council (DPCGC); and

Ombudsman of Federation of Indian Fantasy Sports (FIFS). He is also a visiting Professor at various Law Universities.

Justice Sikri has been conferred Doctorate of Laws, Honoris Causa, by National Law University Delhi on 31 August 2018 and by Dr. Ram Manohar Lohiya National Law University, Lucknow, in November 2013. He started his practice at the Delhi High Court in 1977 and handled all types of cases, with specialisation in Arbitration, Commercial, Labour, and Constitutional matters. He was counsel for various public sector undertakings, banks, and financial institutions. He taught Law at the Campus Law Centre from 1984 to 1989. In 1997, he was designated a Senior Advocate by the Delhi High Court, and in 1999, became a judge of the Delhi High Court, and in 2011, its Acting Chief Justice. In September 2012, he was elevated as the Chief Justice of the Punjab & Haryana High Court, and in April 2013, he was appointed as a judge of the Supreme Court. He superannuated in March 2019 as the senior-most puisne judge.

Justice Sikri has authored over 4700 reported judgments in different fields of law. He was chosen as one of the 50 most influential persons in the world who impacted the growth of Intellectual Property Laws for the year 2007 by Managing Intelletual Property Association (MIPA). He has authored scholarly articles in various journals and presented papers at many national and international conferences. He has several articles in the field of human rights, commercial laws, arbitration, and mediation. After his retirement, he is undertaking Opinion work, Mediation, as well as Arbitration – both domestic and international.

Justice through a New Lens

In Re: Recruitment of Visually Impaired in Judicial Services v. The Registrar General, High Court of Madhya Pradesh

Justice Rekha Palli

Introduction: A Courtroom of One's Own

The Indian judiciary has long been a beacon of hope for the marginalised, and in that line, its recent judgment *In Re: Recruitment of Visually Impaired in Judicial Services v. The Registrar General, High Court of Madhya Pradesh,*[1] marks a watershed moment in disability rights jurisprudence. On 3 March 2025, the Supreme Court of India, vide the said decision, struck down provisions of the Madhya Pradesh Judicial Service (Recruitment and Conditions of Service) Rules, 1994, which were found to be discriminatory against Persons with Disabilities (PwD). In doing so, the court undertook a comprehensive examination of the rights of disabled persons vis-à-vis the principles of equality as enshrined in the Constitution of India. The present article attempts to delve into the various issues discussed in this landmark decision and analyse how the court has addressed the different dimensions of the principle of equality.

1. 2025 SCC OnLine SC 481

The Case that Changed Everything

This case originated from a letter petition dated 15 January 2024, written by the mother of a visually impaired judicial aspirant, questioning the legality of the Madhya Pradesh Judicial Service Examination (Recruitment and Conditions of Service) Rules, 1994, as amended on 23 June 2023. Rule 6A of the amended rules excluded visually impaired and low-vision candidates from judicial appointments. The Petitioner contended that such exclusion was arbitrary, discriminatory, and in violation of the spirit of the Constitution, particularly the principles enshrined in the Rights of Persons with Disabilities Act, 2016 (RPwD Act, 2016).

On 7 March 2024, the Supreme Court took *suo motu* cognisance of the letter petition, leading to Suo Motu Writ Petition (C) No. 6/2024. Additionally, a visually impaired law student from Rajasthan also petitioned the Chief Justice of India, highlighting similar issues in Rajasthan's Judicial Services Examination. Since these matters raised similar questions of law and underscored the broader systemic exclusion of visually impaired candidates across different states, they were considered together.

Separately, an appeal, being SLP(C) No. 12179/2024, was filed against the Madhya Pradesh High Court's decision in WP No. 30465 of 2023, wherein the High Court had upheld the amendment to Rule 7 of the 1994 recruitment rules and the subsequent advertisement dated 17 November 2023 issued by it. In addition to the fundamental requirements, such as Indian citizenship and an LLB degree, the amendment introduced certain additional conditions for appearing in the Rajasthan Judicial Services examination. It mandated that the candidates must either have three years of practice at the Bar or have passed all examinations in the first attempt with a minimum aggregate score of 70% for General and Other Backward Class (OBC) categories and 50% for Scheduled Caste (SC) and Scheduled Tribe (ST) categories. Similarly, the advertisement dated 17 November 2023 clarified that to qualify for the exemption from the three-year practice requirement, candidates must have cleared all examinations without appearing in any supplementary exams or utilising the Allowed to Keep Terms (ATKT) provision. The challenge sought an exemption for persons with disabilities, arguing that the failure to provide accommodations was legally untenable.

The Petitioner highlighted that while an able-bodied person may not face much difficulty in fulfilling the mandatory three-year practice rule, the principle of reasonable accommodation requires acknowledging that the infrastructure of most Indian courts is not disablilty compliant. Therefore, even though a PwD candidate may have the mental abilities to perform judicial functions, they may struggle with the level of physical activity required for legal practice, which could, in turn, hinder their ability to fulfil this mandatory requirement.

The Supreme Court was, thus, faced with a pivotal question: Could disability, per se, be a ground for disqualification from judicial services, or did the law mandate a more inclusive and accommodative approach?

Key Legal Issues

1. Whether visually impaired candidates can be said to be 'not suitable' for judicial services.

2. Whether the amendment made in Rule 6A of Madhya Pradesh Judicial Services (Recruitment and Conditions of Service) Rules, 1994, falls foul of the Constitution.

3. Whether the proviso to Rule 7 of the Madhya Pradesh Judicial Service (Recruitment and Conditions of Service) Rules, 1994,

violates the equality doctrine and the principle of reasonable accommodation.

4. Whether relaxation can be granted in assessing the suitability of candidates when adequate PwD candidates are not available after selection in their respective categories.

5. Whether a separate cut-off is required to be maintained and selection conducted accordingly for visually impaired candidates.[2]

Core Takeaways from the Decision

Constitutionalising Disability Rights: The Need for Fundamental Recognition

The Indian Constitution enshrines inclusivity and equality through Articles 14, 15, and 16. While Article 14 of the Constitution encapsulates the general principle of equality, Article 15 enumerates specific grounds for non-discrimination. It, however, does not mention disability. This omission has long been criticised, including by the UN Committee on the Rights of Persons with Disabilities (2019). While the RPwD Act, 2016, enacted under Article 253 of the Constitution, provides statutory protections akin to those provided for socially and educationally backward classes, constitutional recognition for the rights of the PwD remains crucial. With 70 countries explicitly protecting the rights of the disabled in their constitutions, India must follow suit. The RPwD Act, 2016, now recognised as a 'super-statute', has reshaped public and legal discourse, reinforcing the urgent need for constitutionalising disability rights as a fundamental right.[3]

---

2. *Id.*, para 29.1

3. *Id.*, para 36

Judicial Approach: Progress made thus Far

The court took note of the evolution of disability rights jurisprudence in India, recognising the judiciary's pivotal role in advancing the rights of persons with disabilities. Over the years, the Supreme Court of India has played a transformative role in shaping the legal framework for the rights of persons with disabilities.

In *Union of India v. National Federation of Blind*,[4] the court recognised that ensuring employment is crucial for the empowerment of PwD, stressing that social and practical barriers, rather than the disability itself, exclude them from the workforce. Similarly, in *Jeeja Ghosh v. Union of India*,[5] the court highlighted the need for reasonable differentiation, ensuring that PwD receive the necessary accommodations to achieve substantive equality as enshrined under the Constitution.

The principle of reasonable accommodation was reinforced in *Vikash Kumar v. UPSC*,[6] where the court held that the State and private entities have a positive obligation to provide additional support to PwD, ensuring their full and effective participation in society. The judgment emphasised that without such support, fundamental rights under Articles 14, 19, and 21 of the Constitution of India would remain hollow. Similarly, in *Rajive Raturi v. Union of India*,[7] the court directed strict compliance with the Rights of Persons with Disabilities (RPwD) Act, 2016, mandating the removal of infrastructural barriers to ensure accessibility. Further, in *Justice Sunanda Bhandare Foundation v. Union of India*,[8] the court admonished executive lethargy, directing that government action

4. (2013) 10 SCC 772
5. (2016) 7 SCC 761
6. (2021) 5 SCC 370
7. (2018) 2 SCC 413
8. (2014) 14 SCC 383

should be relief-oriented rather than obstructive in implementing disability rights.

The right to dignity, a cornerstone of Article 21, has been central to the court's reasoning. In *Francis Coralie Mullin v. Administrator, Union Territory of Delhi*,[9] the court held that any act impairing human dignity constitutes a deprivation of the right to life. This reasoning was extended in *Ravinder Kumar Dhariwal v. Union of India*,[10] where the court recognised disability as a social construct, arguing that one-size-fits-all solutions are inadequate given the diverse barriers faced by individuals. The mandate for protecting PwD is also reinforced through Article 41 of the Constitution of India, which directs the State to make effective provisions for public assistance to disabled persons. As emphasised in *Jacob M. Puthuparambil v. Kerala Water Authority*,[11] courts must interpret laws in such a way that advances the spirit of Article 41. Moreover, India's obligations under the United Nations Convention on the Rights of Persons with Disabilities (UNCRPD) further strengthen the need to ensure that reasonable accommodation is not a privilege but an enforceable right, essential for ensuring equality and non-discrimination for the PwD.

Adopting a Rights-based Approach

The court adopted a rights-based approach and emphasised the concepts of positive rights, affirmative action, and reasonable accommodation. The RPwD Act, 2016, embodies the principle of reasonable accommodation, ensuring that a PwD's suitability and capability are assessed not through clinical assessments but in an enabling environment. The court, relying on its earlier decision

9. (1981) 1 SCC 608

10. (2023) 2 SCC 209

11. (1991) 1 SCC 28

in *Vikash Kumar* wherein it was held that ignoring reasonable accommodation amounts to disability-based discrimination and conflict with the ideal of inclusive equality, noted, 'The principle of reasonable accommodation captures the positive obligation of the State and private parties to provide additional support to persons with disabilities to facilitate their full and effective participation in society...'[12]

The court, therefore, held that Clause 6A of the Madhya Pradesh Judicial Service Examination Rules, 1994, which bars visually impaired candidates based on medical assessments, violates not only the principle of substantive equality enshrined under the RPwD Act but is also in contravention of India's international obligations. The court observed that UNCRPD Committee's General Comment No. 6 reinforces that disability is a social construct, rejecting the medical model as a basis for restricting rights. Visually impaired candidates, having completed a law degree, must not be arbitrarily excluded from judicial service. Further, observing that the principle of legitimate expectation strengthens the claim of the petitioners, the court held that Rule 6A of the recruitment rules is unconstitutional and inconsistent with the evolving disability jurisprudence on this count too.[13]

Striking down Structural Discrimination

Observing that the constitutional courts must enforce equality, 'by adopting a rights-based approach, providing an enabling environment and atmosphere, and ensuring that PwD are provided with equal opportunities, and accommodation that they need and deserve in order to make sure that they can lead their lives with dignity, realising their fullest potential without

---

12. *Supra* note 1, para 40 (iii)

13. *Id.*, para 42

facing discrimination,'[14] the court struck down the exclusionary recruitment policy as being violative of both statutory and constitutional provisions, reinforcing that the judiciary, as an institution, must lead by example in upholding inclusivity.

Role of Assistive Technology in Judicial Functions: 'It Can Be Done'

The court differentiated between 'eligibility' and 'suitability', rightly recognising that the latter is determined by how an individual performs the various functions associated with a post, which, in turn, is influenced by external factors. Recognising the rapid advancements in technology, the court underscored the efficacy of assistive tools such as screen readers, Artificial Intelligence (AI)-driven legal research applications, and digital case management systems. It cited instances of visually impaired judges globally who have successfully discharged judicial duties, 'showcasing that visual impairment does not preclude one's ability to make significant contributions to the field of law.'[15] The judgment directed authorities to adopt necessary technological interventions to enable equal participation in judicial services.

Understanding the Impact of the Decision

The Supreme Court's decision *In Re: Recruitment of Visually Impaired in Judicial Services* is significant for disability rights jurisprudence as the court unequivocally held that visually impaired individuals cannot be excluded from judicial services merely on account of their disability. In coming to this conclusion, the court emphasised that the principle of equality is based on inclusivity and substantive equality.

It is further noteworthy that in order to adequately assess the

14. *Id.*, para 3

15. *Id.*, para 66

impact of its decision on PwD, the court deemed it proper to call upon Dr. Sanjay S. Jain, a professor of Law at the National Law School of India University, Bangalore, who has over 25 years of teaching experience and is totally blind since birth, as an intervenor. The court, therefore, displayed a truly inclusive approach in not just its observations but also in the process through which the same were arrived at.

Shift from the Medical Model to the Social Model of Disability

The court critically examined the evolving understanding of disability, highlighting the need to adopt a more inclusive and progressive perspective. The medical model or the 'tragedy' model perceives disability as a condition that requires treatment akin to a disease. The social model of disability, which emerged in response to the limitations of the medical model, is grounded in the difference between an 'impairment' and 'disability'. It recognises that while an impairment is a medical phenomenon, disability is a social construct, shaped by external factors.

The judgment, taking note of the same, emphasised the need to move away from the medical model of disability to the social model, recognising the need to eliminate the paternalistic and patronising approach taken toward PwD.

Indirect Discrimination, Substantive Equality, and Reasonable Accommodation

Equality, which has long been recognised as a basic feature of the Constitution, is not merely a negative right. The idea of equality under Article 14 of the Constitution encompasses real and substantive equality, which strikes at the inequities arising out of social and economic factors.[16] The State is under a Constitutional

16. *Secretary, HSEB v. Suresh*, AIR 1999 SC 1160

mandate to ensure equality in access to opportunities for all. This mandate is not an empty formality; it extends beyond non-discrimination and requires positive actions to create a society where persons with disabilities can participate fully and without barriers. It is, therefore, the State's duty to foster an enabling and inclusive environment for persons with disabilities.

In Re: Recruitment of Visually Impaired in Judicial Services, the court expounded upon the concept of indirect discrimination, noting that while some decisions may appear to be facially neutral, the impact thereof is so as to discriminate against one particular group of citizens or identities. Taking note of the international jurisprudence on indirect discrimination, the court observed that in the present case, the effect of the impugned rules was such that it burdened candidates with physical disabilities, thereby negating substantive equality.

The court's observations qua the principle of indirect discrimination and its effect on substantive equality reaffirm the fundamental principle of equality as enshrined in the Constitution of India, i.e., unequals cannot be treated equally, and sometimes equal treatment may lead to unequal results.

Further, recognising that disability does not operate in isolation, the court acknowledged that a person who is suffering from multiple disabilities would perhaps require a greater degree of accommodation. In this context, the court underscored the importance of adopting a more holistic and inclusive approach toward PwD. The decision, therefore, reiterated that equality and inclusivity demand reasonable accommodation, i.e., accommodation that is tailored to the requirements of each condition of disability.

Thus, the Supreme Court's ruling not only brings India's disability rights jurisprudence in consonance with the international legal framework, particularly the UNCRPD, to which India is a signatory, but also reinforces the Constitutional mandate of ensuring equality in access to public opportunities.

Conclusion

This verdict will certainly act as a catalyst for systemic change, paving the way for visually impaired law graduates to aspire for judicial positions without fear of arbitrary exclusion. By incorporating diversity, the judiciary gains nuanced perspectives that enrich judicial reasoning and promote a broader, more inclusive interpretation of law, and clearly mandates a shift from a model of exclusion to one of integration. The judgment marks a pivotal moment in India's disability rights movement, ensuring that ability, not disability, defines a judge's competence and, therefore, challenges societal perceptions of disability and reinforces the idea that justice must be accessible to all.

It is often said that the true measure of a democracy is in how it treats its most marginalised. The ruling signals the dawn of a judiciary that truly embodies the principle of justice for all—the kind of justice that is blind only in its impartiality, not in its inclusivity. It would, therefore, not be inappropriate to say that the Supreme Court's decision *In Re: Recruitment of Visually Impaired in Judicial Services* is more than a judicial pronouncement—it is a transformative vision for an inclusive legal system and society. The judgment's ramifications would surely extend beyond the judiciary, establishing a precedent that public employment must be assessed on the basis of capability rather than outdated stereotypes.

Justice Rekha Palli

Justice Rekha Palli is a former Judge of the Delhi High Court with a career in law spanning several decades. Prior to her elevation to the Bench in 2017, she practised extensively before the Supreme Court and various High Courts, developing expertise in the complex and often sensitive domain of service and military matters. She made significant contributions to service law jurisprudence and appeared in several landmark cases involving the Armed Forces.

A significant chapter in her illustrious career involved spearheading the legal battle for gender equality in the Armed Forces. Her unwavering advocacy and passion for gender justice culminated in the landmark judgment of the Delhi High Court in *Babita Puniya v. The Secretary, Ministry of Defence* which resulted in the grant of permanent commission to women in the Armed Forces on being upheld by the Supreme Court. The judgment marks a milestone in the evolution of gender rights in India, reaffirming the constitutional promise of equality and non-discrimination.

As a judge, she authored several significant judgments spanning diverse areas of law, including administrative law, commercial law, family law, service matters, and motor accident claims. Some of her noteworthy decisions include *Sachin Arora v. Manju Arora*, where she examined the contours of the right to privacy in the context of adultery; a Full Bench decision in *Dr. Geetanjali Agarwal v. Dr. Manoj Agarwal*, which held that interlocutory orders passed under the Guardians and Wards Act, 1890, are appealable under the Family Courts Act, 1984; and the landmark five-Judge Bench judgment in *Saif Ali @ Sohan v. GNCTD*, which balanced the accused's right to a speedy trial with the victim's right to compensation under Section 357 of the Code of Criminal Procedure (CrPC)—marking a significant advancement in victim-centric criminal jurisprudence.

Having retired from the Delhi High Court, Justice Rekha Palli now practices in the Supreme Court of India as a Senior Advocate.

The Conundrum over the Guardianship of Comatose Patients

Shobha Gopalakrishnan v. State of Kerala

Justice Rajive Bhalla

Introduction

Mark Lanegan, an American musician and songwriter, in his memoir *Devil in a Coma,* wrote about his experience undergoing treatment for coronavirus disease 2019 (COVID-19) in March 2021. He was overcome by the illness and was unable to move and function for several months, slipping in and out of a comatose state. He eventually passed away in 2022. In the hospital, Lanegan, once known for his dry humour and his performances as a lead for the rock band Screaming Trees, and half a dozen albums, now held the record for surviving the longest in this state.[1] In his powerful memoir that he wrote during this time, he notes:

1. Kitty Empire, '*Devil in a Coma* by Mark Lanegan – a rockstar collides with Covid', *The Guardian*, 10 January 2022, available at: https://www.theguardian.com/books/2022/jan/10/devil-in-a-coma-by-mark-lanegan-review-a-rock-star-collides-with-covid (accessed 1 October 2024)

> It's hard to know where you are when you're trying to read a map by the light of a falling star.[2]

This essay will discuss a serious and important issue. A statutory lacuna, which has come up time and again before several High Courts of India, namely the Kerala High Court, the Allahabad High Court, the Delhi High Court, and the Bombay High Court. The essay shall breakdown the decision delivered by the Kerala High Court in *Shobha Gopalkrishnan v. State of Kerala & Others*,[3] a judgment by two Judges of the Kerala High Court that highlights the plight of a family physically, and financially exhausted while looking after their comatose bread earner but unable to access his bank accounts and property to pay his bills since the Parliament omitted to legislate for such situations. The judgment also highlights how the Kerala High Court invoked a rarely used doctrine of law and issued directions to alleviate the misery of the petitioners.

The decision of the Kerala High Court in *Shobha Gopalkrishnan* restores the author's faith in the social commitment of the judiciary of India. This essay is as much about disability or inability as it is about ability; the ability of two Judges of the Kerala High Court, P.R. Ramachandra and N. Anil Kumar, to grant relief where the statute is silent, the ability of the court to invoke a doctrine so fundamental to the cause of justice that it gets lost in the maze of the daily humdrum of law namely the doctrine of *causes omissus* and as explained in this judgment; 'courts have to do what the parliament would have done'. This essay is also about the resilience of a family exhausted physically and financially, while looking after their comatose breadwinner, but unable to access his bank accounts or monetise his property for want

---

2. Mark Lanegan, *Devil in a Coma – A Memoir* (White Rabbit Publications, 14 December 2021)

3. 2019 SCC OnLine Ker 739

of a law appointing them as guardians. Turned away from every door they approached, the High Court of Kerala put forth their plight and adjudicated the issue of the appointment of a guardian to access bank accounts and property.

The Case

The Petitioners in the abovementioned case were the wife and son of Shri T. Gopalakrishnan. Shri Gopalakrishnan, who had suffered irreversible brain damage on account of a cardiac arrest, lay in a permanent vegetative state and coma since 28 April 2018. The Petitioners, facing extreme financial hardship and having spent a huge sum of money on the patient's treatment, now prayed before the Kerala High Court to appoint the first Petitioner, i.e., the wife of the patient, as his Legal Guardian. They further submitted that the biggest hurdle to the said prayer was the legal quagmire they found themselves in. Suprisingly, as per the Petitioner, their circumstances were peculiar to the statutory provisions relating to Guardianship and submitted that neither the Guardian and Wards Act, 1890, the National Trust for the Welfare of Persons with Autism, Cerebral Palsy, Mental Retardation and Multiple Disabilities Act, 1999 (hereinafter referred to as National Trust Act), the Mental Health Act, 1987, the Mental Healthcare Act, 2017, nor the Rights of Persons with Disabilities Act, 2016 came to their aid as none of the above dealt with the aspect of appointment of a Guardian of a Comatose Patient. Accordingly, the prayer before the High Court of Kerala was to invoke their powers under Article 226 and declare the Petitioner, the wife of the patient, as the guardian of her husband. Unfortunately, before the matter could be adjudicated, Shri Gopalakrishnan passed away in 2019. The court, now treating the matter as Public Interest Litigation (PIL), decided to deal with several aspects that came before it in this important case.

Faced with multiple dilemmas, the High Court invoked the principle of *casus omissus* read with Article 226 of the Constitution of India.

The Position of Law

The High Court carefully examined the above-mentioned Acts of Parliament in great detail. At the outset, the High Court observed that the Guardians and Wards Act, 1890, dealing with the appointment of guardians for minors, and the Mental Health Act, 1987, providing for the appointment of guardians for 'mentally ill'[4] persons, would not come to the rescue in the present factual matrix. The latter is also because the definition of mental illness as per the Mental Health Act, 1987 only covered in its ambit persons who are in need of treatment of any mental disorder other than mental retardation.[5] For the reason that the patient in a comatose state does not respond to any stimuli and is in a position where there remain no more treatment options, they may not be covered under the statute.

The Mental Health Care Act, 2017, a fairly recent legislation, does provide for the appointment of a 'nominated representative'. It also ensures inclusion of persons with mental illness to participate in ensuring a 'rights-based services delivery' under Section 34(1)(n) and 46(1)(n), whereby two members having mental illness constitute the Mental Health Review Board. However, the statute fell short in coming to the rescue in the present case since the definition of mental illness as per Section 2(s) once again did not include within its ambit a person lying in a comatose state. The National Trust Act fell short in these circumstances as well,

4. Mental Health Act, 1987 (repealed), Section 2(l)

5. *Ibid.*

since a patient in a permanent vegetative state or coma did not fall within the purview of the definition of 'multiple disabilities'[6] to the extent required under the statute. Lastly, the Rights of Persons with Disabilities Act, 2016, also does not come to the aid of the Petitioner as it defines a 'person with disability'[7] as someone who is able to interact with others, even if not entirely; something which is simply not the case for a comatose patient, as there is no interaction or response to stimuli at all.

The Way Out

After a thorough examination and analysis of each of these statutes, the High Court concluded that this matter presented a situation where no remedy was available and invoked its jurisdiction under Article 226 to provide relief to patients in a comatose state. The court noted:

> Considering the role of this court, jurisdiction under Article 226 of the Constitution of India springs up when no remedy is provided under any Statute to persons like patients in jurisdiction. A reference to the verdict in *Nothman v. Barnet London Borough Council*, [1978 (1) WLR 220] (at 228) is also relevant. In such cases, it is often said, courts have to do what the Parliament would have done. A reference to the verdict in *Surjit Singh Kalra v. Union of India* [1991 (2) SCC 87] explaining the principle of *casus omissus* is also brought to the notice of this court; to the effect that if it is an accidental omission, the court can supply/fill up the gap. This court, however, does not find it appropriate to 're-write' the provision, as it is within the exclusive domain of the

6. National Trust Act, 1999, Section 2(h)

7. Rights of Persons with Disability Act, 2016, Section 2(a)

> Parliament. This is more so when the relevant statutes like Mental Health Act, 1987, and the PwD Act, 1995, came to be repealed, on introducing the new legislations, such as the Mental Healthcare Act 2017 and The Rights of Persons with Disabilities Act, 2016, in conformity with the mandate of UN Convention, 2006. This court does not say anything whether any amendment is necessary, also in respect of the National Trust Act for the Welfare of Persons with Autism, Cerebral Palsy, Mental Retardation and Multiple Disabilities Act, 1999, (National Trust Act, 1999) with reference to the UN Convention 2006. It is for the Government to consider and take appropriate steps in this regard, as it is never for the court to encroach into the forbidden field. This court would only like to make it clear that, in so far as the case of a patient lying in 'comatose state' is not covered by any of the statutes, (as discussed above), for appointment of a Guardian, the petitioners are justified in approaching this court seeking to invoke the power under Article 226 of the Constitution of India. It is declared accordingly.[8]

The High Court was conscious of the limitations of its jurisdiction and the fact that it does not have the jurisdiction to read into the law a right to appoint a guardian but then held that as Parliament had omitted to do so, and the doctrine of *casus omissus* empowered the court to alleviate the misery of the Petitioner by exercising powers under Article 226 of the Constitution of India, the court observed and issued the following directions:

> Coming to the incidental aspects; since no specific provision is available in any statutes to deal with the procedure for

8. *Supra* note 3, para 42

such appointment of Guardian to a victim lying in 'comatose state', it is necessary to stipulate some 'Guidelines', based on the inputs gathered by this court from different corners, as suggested by the learned counsel for the petitioners, the learned Government Pleader and also by the learned *Amicus Curiae*, till the field is taken over by proper legislation in this regard. This court finds it appropriate to fix the following norms/guidelines as a temporary measure:

i. Petitioner/s seeking for appointment of Guardian to a person lying in comatose state shall disclose the particulars of the property, both movable and immovable, owned and possessed by the patient lying in comatose state.

ii. The condition of the person lying in comatose state shall be got ascertained by causing him to be examined by a duly constituted Medical Board, of whom one shall definitely be a qualified neurologist.

iii. A simultaneous visit of the person lying in comatose state, at his residence, shall be caused to be made through the Revenue authorities, not below the rank of a Tahsildar and a report shall be procured as to all relatives, their financial conditions and such other aspects.

iv. The person seeking appointment as Guardian of a person lying in comatose state shall be a close relative (spouse or children) and all the persons to be classified as legal heirs in the due course shall be in the party array. In the absence of the suitable close relative, a public official such as 'Social Welfare officer' can be sought to be appointed as a Guardian to the person lying in 'comatose state'.

v. The person applying for appointment as Guardian shall be one who is legally competent to be appointed as a Guardian

vi. The appointment of a Guardian as above shall only be in respect of the specific properties and bank accounts/such other properties of the person lying in comatose state; to be indicated in the order appointing the Guardian and the Guardian so appointed shall act always in the best interest of the person lying in 'comatose state'.

vii. The person appointed as Guardian shall file periodical reports in every six months before the Registrar General of this court, which shall contain the particulars of all transactions taken by the Guardian in respect of the person and property of the patient in comatose state; besides showing the utilization of the funds received and spent by him/her.

viii. The Registrar General shall cause to maintain a separate Register with regard to appointment of Guardian to persons lying in 'comatose state' and adequate provision to keep the Reports filed by the Guardian appointed by this court.

ix. It is open for this court to appoint a person as Guardian to the person lying in comatose state, either temporarily or for a specified period or permanently, as found to be appropriate.

x. If there is any misuse of power or misappropriation of funds or non-extension of requisite care and protection or support with regard to the treatment and other requirements of the person lying in comatose state, it is open to bring up the matter for further consideration of this court to re-open and revoke the power, to take appropriate action against the person concerned, who was appointed as the Guardian and also to appoint another person/public authority/Social Welfare Officer (whose official status is equal to the post of District Probation Officer) as the Guardian.

xi. It shall be for the Guardian appointed by the court to meet the obligations/duties similar to those as described under Section 15 of the National Trust Act and to maintain and submit the accounts similar to those contained in Section 16.

xii. The Guardian so appointed shall bring the appointment to the notice of the Social Welfare Officer having jurisdiction in the place of residence, along with a copy of the verdict appointing him as Guardian, enabling the Social Welfare Officer of the area to visit the person lying in 'comatose state' at random and to submit a report, if so necessitated, calling for further action/ interference of this court.

xiii. The transactions in respect of the property of the person lying in 'comatose state', by the Guardian, shall be strictly in accordance with the relevant provisions of law. If the Guardian appointed is found to be abusing the power or neglects or acts contrary to the best interest of the person lying in 'comatose state', any relative or next friend may apply to this court for removal of such Guardian.

xiv. The Guardian appointed shall seek and obtain specific permission from this court, if he/she intends to transfer the person lying in 'comatose state' from the jurisdiction

> of this court to another State or Country, whether it be for availing better treatment or otherwise.[9]

It is true that a court can neither legislate nor fill gaps in an existing statute, but where the situation so demands, a High Court exercising jurisdiction under Article 226 of the Constitution of India, cannot stand as a mute spectator allowing injustice to prevail. The predicament of the family unable to provide for a comatose member is one such situation where the cause of justice must prevail over judicial constraints. The Kerala High Court deserves praise and support for reading into the law a right to appoint a guardian where the law is silent on such an appointment.

The High Court's decision represents more than a legal victory; it serves as a profound societal statement. The court's willingness to step in where the law fell short not only provides immediate aid, but also sets a precedent which came to be relied upon by several constitutional courts,[10] proving how the decision inspired meaningful change in the lives of those families who are caring for their loved ones in a permanently vegetative state or coma. Even though the present case and many that came after are proof that justice did prevail for the family of those who are comatose, the discussion raises some important questions. One of the most important discussion points herein is whether the law relating to mental and physical disability is inherently discriminatory towards comatose patients inasmuch as none of the statutes find

---

9. *Id.*, para 43

10. *Uma Mittal v. Union of India*, 2020 SCC OnLine ALL 277; *Vandana Tyagi v. Government of NCT of Delhi*, 2020 SCC OnLine Del 32; *Dipaben w/o Dhaval Laximikant Bhatt v. State of Gujarat*, SCA 11390/2021, decided by Gujarat High Court on 20 October 2021; *Vijaylakshmi Acharya & Others v. State of Tamil Nadu*, WP 6926/2021 decided by the High Court of Madras on 17 March 2021; *Anjuben Karansin Dodiya v. State of Gujarat*, SCA 3687/2024 decided by the Gujarat High Court on 22 July 2024

application to those in a coma. Hopefully, this decision serves as a first step in the discussion surrounding the rights of comatose patients, and the law surrounding the issue continues to evolve. By stepping in where legislative gaps exist, the court highlighted a crucial issue that affects countless families. The societal impact of this decision extends beyond the legal realm; it acknowledges the struggles of such families and provides a hopeful path for those who feel abandoned, isolated, and lost.

Unlike T. Gopalakrishnan, Mark Lanegan found himself back from a long coma, albeit for a small duration, eventually passing away within the year. He wrote something in his memoir[11] that the author is compelled to end this essay with, in order to ensure that the discussion around the rights of those in a comatose state does not end with this decision.

> More and more this (his time in and out of the comatose state) was reminiscent of an unending stretch in country jail that I could not shake, with my trial date being intentionally undetermined, constantly moved around just to keep me inside. It felt like the longer I was kept here the worse I got, not the other way around.[12]

11. *Supra* note 2

12. Mark Lanegan, *Devil in a Coma*, available at: https://www.goodreads.com/author/quotes/14952354.Mark_Lanegan?page=2 (accessed 3 August 2024)

Justice Rajive Bhalla

Justice Bhalla's journey through the corridors of courts commenced in 1978 when he joined the Bar of the Punjab and Haryana High Court. He was elevated as a Judge of the same High Court in 2004, beginning a journey that ended in 2016. After retiring from the High Court, he chaired two tribunals simultaneously. On completion of his stint at the tribunals, he switched back to the Bar at the Supreme Court as a Senior Advocate. Justice Bhalla is also the Dean, Department of Law at Guru Nanak Dev University, Amritsar, Punjab. His journey to explore the law continues. He considers himself lucky to be living in the times of great legal challenges and hopes that the good fight for the rights of humans continues.

Streamlining the Admission Process to Medical Institutions for the Disabled

Omkar Ramchandra Gond v. Union of India

Prof. Balram K. Gupta

It has been beautifully expressed: You learn to speak by speaking. To study by studying. To run by running. To work by working. To love by loving. Francis Bacon has said, 'Natural abilities are like natural plants.' Disabilities cannot be converted into natural abilities, but they certainly can be converted from disabilities to abilities. This is the true challenge in every domain, including the medical field.

Healthy disability jurisprudence is the need of the hour. The 'Disability' deserves to be converted into 'Ability'. Of course, to the extent practically and humanly possible. The limitations are understandable. The best way to surmount these limitations is through constant effort and endeavour. This is a continuous exercise. It is in this backdrop that we have the apex court judgment in the case of *Omkar Ramchandra Gond v. Union of India and Others*[1] of

1. 2024 SCC Online SC 2860

15 October 2024. This is a pathbreaking judgment in the domain of admissions to medical institutions, universities, and colleges. The effort on the part of the three-judge bench led by Justice B.R. Gavai, including Justices Aravind Kumar and K.V. Viswanathan, is to provide solutions and to correct the wrongs and missteps of different authorities. This was followed by two more judgments in the same progressive vein, more on those later in this chapter.

The Case

Omkar Ramachandra Gond (the Appellant) grew up in a middle-class family. His father was a government servant. His academic performance was creditable. In the tenth standard, he scored 97.2%. He got 1st division in his school finals. He wanted to be a doctor.

The Appellant had a speech and language disability. He was certified to have 44–45% permanent disability. This was according to the Disability Certificate dated 18 May 2017. The Appellant applied for the National Eligibility cum Entrance Test (NEET-UG) 2024 for admission to the MBBS (Bachelor of Medicine and Bachelor of Surgery) course. His application, dated 18 February 2024, was under the category of Persons with Disability (PwD) and Other Backward Classes (OBC). The application form had a disclaimer clause. It stated that the eligibility under the PwD category was purely provisional. It was to be governed as per the National Medical Commission (NMC) guidelines. The guidelines were regarding the admission of students with 'specified disabilities' under the Rights of Persons with Disabilities Act, 2016 (RPwD) Act.

The Appellant appeared for the NEET held on 5 May 2024. He qualified the entrance examination. As per the Information Brochure, the candidates were required to undergo a medical examination to be conducted by Disability Assessment Board.

The Appellant approached the designated Disability Certification Centre on 16 August 2024. The Certification Centre certified that the Appellant had a 44% disability. The Board of Governors of the Medical Council of India had amended the Graduate Medical Education Regulations, 1997, vide notification dated 13 May 2019. According to the amended Regulations, persons with less than 40% disability were eligible for medical courses but not eligible for the reservation quota for PwD. Thus, the Disability Certification Centre declared that the Appellant was not eligible to pursue the medical course as per NMC norms.

The Appellant moved the High Court at Bombay with a writ petition contending that the Medical Council of India/NMC is not empowered to lay down eligibility criteria in such a manner as to take away the benefits under the RPwD Act. The Appellant also challenged the notification dated 13 May 2019 as also the Certificate issued by the Disability Certification Centre, vide which he had been rendered ineligible for pursuing the medical course. The Appellant also sought interim relief to permit him to participate in the centralised admission process. The High Court simply adjourned the matter to 19 September 2024. It did not pass any interim order.

The last date for submitting the choice for admission was 29 August 2024. The results of the CAP Round-I were to be declared on 30 August 2024. The Appellant moved the Supreme Court seeking urgent relief. The matter came up before the apex court on 2 September 2024. After hearing the counsel for the NMC, the court passed an order directing:

i. The seat to which the Appellant would have been entitled, if rendered eligible, be kept vacant.

ii. The Dean, Government Medical College and Sassoon General Hospital, Pune, to constitute a Medical Board consisting of one or more specialist(s) having domain expertise pertaining to the Appellant's disability. The Medical Board was to specifically examine whether the speech and language disability of the Appellant would come in way of his pursuing the MBBS course.

The said medical college did not have the facility. Therefore, the task was entrusted to Maulana Azad Medical College, Delhi. The Medical Board gave the opinion and reported that the Appellant's speech and language disability would not come in the way of the Appellant in pursuing the MBBS course. The Supreme Court, after hearing the counsel for different parties, passed this order on 18 September 2024: 'For the reasons to be recorded separately, the appeal is allowed. The Appellant is directed to be admitted against the seat which was directed to be kept vacant as per the orders passed by this court.' The detailed judgment was later released on 15 October 2024. This judgment has laid down the roadmap for admissions to medical courses under the PwD category.

The Road Map for PwD Admissions Unfolds

The top court examined the question: Merely because the disability is quantified at 44%/45%, should the Appellant be disqualified from obtaining admission under the PwD category for the MBBS course?

The Disabilities (Equal Opportunities, Protection of Rights and Full Participation) Act, 1995, was replaced with the Rights of Persons with Disabilities Act, 2016 (RPwD). The Act of 2016 was reflective of the United Nations Convention on the Rights of Persons with Disabilities. The RPwD Act has a number of salutary provisions. Under Section 32, it provides for the reservation of not less than 5% of seats for persons with benchmark disabilities. This reservation was applicable to all government institutions of higher education and other higher education institutions receiving aid from the government. The Appellant was seeking admission under the 5% reservation quota. According to the relevant Regulations, persons with less than 40% disability were not eligible for the PwD quota, but they were otherwise eligible to pursue the medical course. This was a strange situation. With the same benchmark disability, one was entitled to pursue the medical course but was not eligible to avail of the reservation quota. There could possibly be no reasonable rationale for the same. In this context, the top court held that merely because of the quantification of the disability for speech and language at 40% or above, a candidate does not forfeit his or her right to stake a claim for admission for the course of his or her choice. The Regulations are treating unequals equally. The court opined that lumping together persons with benchmark disabilities would be violative of Article 14 of the Constitution. Resultantly, it was held that the Regulations of the Medical Council cannot be interpreted to mean that merely because of the quantification of the disability percentage exceeding the prescribed limits, a person automatically becomes ineligible for the medical course.

It is relevant to refer to *Vidhi Himmat Katariya v. State of Gujarat and Others.*[2] The Petitioner students had prayed to treat them eligible for reservation under the PwD category and grant them admission to the MBBS course. The Petitioners were suffering from 'Locomotor Disability'. The three-judge bench held:

> Therefore, when the experts in the field had opined against the petitioners, the court would not be justified in sitting over as an appellate authority against the opinion formed by the experts.[3]

2. (2019) 10 SCC 20

3. *Id.*, para 8

In *Gond's* case, the Supreme Court adopted a different approach. It held: 'The approach of the Government, instrumentalities of States, regulatory bodies, and for that matter even the private sector, should be as to how best one can accommodate and grant the opportunity to the candidates with disability. The approach should not be about how best to disqualify the candidates and make it difficult for them to pursue and realise their educational goals.'[4] Such positivity of mind of experts will make all the difference. To put it simply, how best the candidate can be helped! How best the disability can be converted into the ability to pursue the MBBS course!

It is with this mindset that the court examined the entire matter at length and in depth. All possible aspects were given due consideration. In this context, the Supreme Court recorded:

> Disabilities Assessment Boards are not monotonous automations to just look at the quantified benchmark disability as set out in the certificate of disability and cast aside the candidate. Such an approach would be antithetical to Article 14 and Article 21 and all canons of justice, equity and good conscience. It will also defeat the statutory objectives of the RPwD Act.[5]

The top court did not stop at this. It further directed that the Disabilities Assessment Boards are obliged to examine the further question as to whether the candidate, in the opinion of the experts in the field, is eligible to pursue the course or, in other words, whether the disability will or will not come in the way of the candidate pursuing the course in question. Still further, it was made clear that the Disability Assessment Boards should state reasons in

---

4. *Supra* note 1, para 38

5. *Id.*, para 46

the event of the Board concluding that the candidate is not eligible to pursue the course.

The Supreme Court did not leave anything to doubt. The Board will have to record reasons for its findings. The reasoned findings will provide a safeguard against arbitrary rejections. Recording of reasons is integral to the principles of natural justice. In any case, the disabled candidates are entitled to reasonable, just, and fair consideration. This is the constitutional mandate. Boards have to discharge their responsibility, not as a formality. They have to ensure that justice is done. The disabled fraternity is entitled to complete justice. Complete justice is a constitutional mandate under Article 142. In fact, complete justice is constitutional morality.

The second issue was regarding the 'one-size-fits-all' theory. This theory came for consideration before the apex court in the case of *Ravinder Kumar Dhariwal v. Union of India,*[6] wherein it observed:

> ...the one-size-fits-all approach can never be used to identify the disability of a person. Disability is not universal but is an individualistic conception based on the impairment that a person has along with the barriers that they face.[7]

This aspect also came for consideration before the apex court in the case of *Bambhaniya Sagar Vasharambhai v. Union of India.*[8] It recorded, 'In the opinion of this court, in cases even of specified disabilities, in all cases the standard of 40% may result in the "one-size-fits-all" norm which will exclude eligible candidates. The Union, therefore, shall consider the steps to mitigate such

6. (2023) 2 SCC 209

7. *Id.,* para 77

8. (2023) SCC Online SC 2173

anomalies....'[9] The National Commission and the Central Government were directed to consider the problem and work out suitable solutions to enable effective participation. Keeping in view these directions, the Ministry of Social Justice and Empowerment issued a communication dated 25 January 2024 to the NMC.

The third issue pertained to the developments in aids and assistive devices and also other technologies that are capable of reducing the effects of disability. In this context, the above-said communication of the government required the NMC to ensure that the statutory requirements of the RPwD Act are followed in letter and spirit. This leaves no doubt that the NMC must take into consideration the developments that can mitigate the disability aspect of PwD.

The fourth issue focuses on the principle of 'Reasonable Accommodation'. This should come into full play. Section 2(y) of the RPwD Act defines Reasonable Accommodation as 'necessary and appropriate modification and adjustments, without imposing a disproportionate and undue burden in a particular case, to ensure to persons with disabilities the enjoyment or exercise or rights equally with others.' The court pointed out that a broad interpretation of the concept of reasonable accommodation, which will further the objective of the RPwD Act and Article 41 of the Indian Constitution - the Directive Principles of State Policy, is mandated. The concept of reasonable accommodation came for judicial interpretation in *Vikash Kumar v. UPSC.*[10] It held: 'The principle of reasonable accommodation captures the positive obligation of the state and private parties to provide additional support to persons with disabilities to facilitate their full and effective participation in society.'[11]

9. *Id.,* para 13

10. (2021) 5 SCC 370

11. *Id.,* para 44

This would, in turn, ensure the Fundamental Rights of equality and right to life of PwD. In fact, the Supreme Court has made it clear that in the matter of providing relief to those who are disabled, the approach and attitude of the executive must be liberal and relief-oriented and not obstructive or lethargic. In another case, *Jeeja Ghosh v. Union of India*,[12] it was observed: 'In concrete terms, it means embracing the notion of positive rights, affirmative action, and reasonable accommodation.'[13] This is the most wholesome approach. If translated into action, it can go a long way in dealing with many issues relating to disabled persons.

The fifth issue pertains to the concept of 'Inclusive Education'. Section 2(m) defines it: Inclusive Education means 'a system of education wherein students with and without disability learn together and the system of teaching and learning is suitably adapted to meet the learning needs of different types of students with disabilities.'

The Convention on Rights of Persons with Disabilities recognises that inclusive education systems must be put in place. This would be a meaningful realisation of the right to education for PwD. The Right to Education is essentially a right to inclusive education. Article 41 casts a duty on the State to make effective provisions for ensuring the right to work, to education, and to public assistance in case of unemployment, old age, sickness, and disablement. Inclusive Education and workplaces will bring in a feeling of fraternity amongst PwD. Both for education and the workplace, the environment of 'inclusiveness' is required. This would navigate 'togetherness' and 'oneness' amongst the disabled and others. They are a part of the same human family. Their life journey covering educational institutions and different workplaces

---

12. (2016) 7 SCC 761

13. *Id.*, para 40

will bring in a spark, a hope, and a sense of accomplishment. This can be achieved not merely through the vehicles of laws but a change of mindset through innovative planning and execution.

In view of the Government of India communication dated 25 January 2024, the NMC has been directed to formulate new regulations/guidelines before the publication of the Admission Brochure for the academic year 2025–26. The regulations will also make provision for the creation of the Appellate Body. The Disability Assessment Boards, which give a negative opinion, will be open to challenge before the constitutional courts. In turn, the court could refer the case to any premier medical institute for an independent opinion. Depending on the opinion, the court will grant the relief. This is how the Appellant got the relief in this case. It is evident that this judgment has carved out a way for medical college admissions for PwD. In fact, admissions to different disciplines. It is translating Article 41 into action. The balance sheet has been prepared. The authorities know what they are required to do and what steps they have to follow. Equally, PwD also know what they can genuinely ask for so that they can get reasonable, just, and fair consideration for admission.

Continuing the Good Work: *Om Rathod Case*

Close to this judgment of 15 October 2024, we have another judgment of a three-judge bench led by the then Chief Justice of India (CJI) Justice Dr. D.Y. Chandrachud and Justices J.B. Pardiwala and Manoj Mishra in the case of *Om Rathod v. Director General of Health Services*[14] rendered on 25 October 2024. This judgment has further solidified the earlier judgment. In fact, it has further strengthened and woven the entire admission process. It has become a self-sufficient code.

14. (2024) SCC OnLine 3130

Om Rathod, the Appellant, had a lower limb locomotor disability. He was academically a good student. He secured an A-I grade in his matriculation and Class XII examination conducted by the Central Board of Secondary Education (CBSE). He appeared for the NEET-UG examination in 2024. The Appellant had secured the All-India PwD Rank of 84 and the State Rank of 4. The eligibility requirement was that persons with over 80% disability may be admitted to a medical course on a case-by-case basis after assessing their functional competence to navigate academic and practical requirements. The Medical Board of AIIMS, Nagpur, vide its certificate dated 13 August 2024, certified that the Appellant was 88% disabled and was declared ineligible to pursue the MBBS course.

The Appellant filed a writ petition before the Nagpur Bench of the High Court of Bombay. He challenged the NEET Disability Certificate issued by AIIMS, Nagpur. The High Court dismissed the writ petition vide its judgment dated 3 September 2024. The Appellant challenged the impugned judgment by filing a Special Leave Petition before the Supreme Court. The top court directed the Appellant to appear before a Medical Board in Delhi. He was to be reassessed, keeping in mind the circular of 24 March 2022. The circular required that a doctor or health professional with disability be included in every Board. The Board gave its report on 9 October 2024. The finding was that there were no changes in most disability components despite the use of assistive devices. The report also made it clear that there were no clear guidelines available to assess the disability with assistive devices. The report was a mere benchmark evaluation report. The disability of the Appellant was brought down from 88% to 80%. The Appellant shared his experience in an affidavit. The approach was negative and obstructive. This experience of the Appellant was reflective of the mindset. Probably, even the association of a doctor with disability could not help. The association of such a doctor was supposed to boost issues related to PwD and bring a balance in assessing the disability, as well as actively assist and aid in the whole assessment process. In short, to give a 'level' consideration, he/she was expected to ensure that the negative approach was eschewed.

The court, in view of *Gond's* case, requested Dr. Satindra Singh of *Infinity Ability* to assist the court in this matter. Dr. Singh carried out a functional assessment after the preliminary conversation with the Appellant. In carrying out the whole exercise, the Appellant was made comfortable. The report finally declared him 'suitable', with appropriate clinical accommodations, to pursue the MBBS course. The detailed report inspires confidence. On 25 October 2024, the apex court directed that the Appellant be permitted to participate in the ongoing counseling process. The top court further directed that a supernumerary seat shall be created at the AIIMS, Nagpur, and the seat shall be allocated to the Appellant. The necessary directions were given to issue fresh guidelines.

These two judgments have effectively conducted a constructive open-heart surgery into the entire admission process and the working of Disability Assessment Boards relating to admissions to medical courses under the category of PwD. The two judgments will certainly streamline the process. They raise hope. PwD can certainly look forward to a medical career. They would be an integral part of serving humanity.

In the second case, *Om Rathod*, while giving the background, the highest court of the land has captured the journey of the Appellant in reaching the top court. It merits reproduction: 'The Appellant has undergone a crash course in navigating the Indian legal system – from statutory prescriptions, regulatory stipulations, High Court adjudication, regulatory and ordered disability assessments to the race to justice before this court.'

This spirit is again reiterated and followed in the recently delivered judgment by the Supreme Court on 21 February 2025 in *Anmol v. Union of India*.[15] Through this verdict, Justices B.R. Gavai and K.V. Viswanathan have reinforced their commitment to inclusive education for Persons with Disabilities. The court criticised the NMC's existing guidelines for their rigid and mechanical application, which often rendered otherwise qualified candidates ineligible for medical courses. Emphasising the need for a functional assessment over a mere quantification of disability, the court mandated that the NMC revise its guidelines to align with the principles of reasonable accommodation and inclusivity as enshrined in the RPwD Act, 2016. This directive builds upon the earlier decision in *Omkar Ramchandra Gond*, highlighting the judiciary's ongoing efforts to ensure that medical admission processes are equitable and just for all candidates, regardless of their disabilities.

This truly is the challenge of disability jurisprudence. If these three judgments are implemented in letter and spirit, the journey from joining the medical course to serving humanity would be smooth and rewarding.

Some Inspiring Stories

The story of Dr. Suresh Advani is worth emulating. He contracted polio at the age of eight. Ever since, he has been on a wheelchair. He started Haematopoietic Stem Cell Transplantation in India. His contributions to the field of Oncology have been recognised with many awards, including *Padma Shree* in 2002 and *Padma Bhushan* in 2012.[16]

---

15. 2025 SCC OnLine SC 387

16. Ullekh NP, 'Meet Dr. Suresh Advani: India's first and best-known Oncologist' *The Economic Times* (22 July 2013), available at: https://economictimes.indiatimes.com/meet-dr-suresh-advani-indias-first-and-best-known-oncologist/articleshow/21245370.cms?from=mdr (accessed 11 December 2024)

It needs to be understood that 'Disability does not mean Inability'. We see so many people already practicing medicine with disabilities. Feranmi Okanlami was in his third year of medical residency at Yale's New Haven Hospital in 2013. He met with an accident while jumping into a swimming pool. He injured his spinal cord and became partially paralysed. The rehabilitation took some time. He returned to practice. He is now a family medicine doctor at the University of Michigan.[17] Lisa Meeks, a psychologist and researcher at Michigan Medicine, specialises in disabilities in medicine and medical education. She co-founded a group focused on improving access to medical education for students with disabilities. Such groups in India can help many by making medical education accessible to them. Meeks also started a Social Media Campaign with the Hashtag – Docs with Disabilities (DwD).[18] She wanted 20 doctors to share their stories online. She was flooded with interest from DwD. There was no end in sight. Erica Dwyer was an internal medicine resident at Cambridge Health in Boston. She was deaf in one ear. She had almost completed her medical school. She realised that she would also lose hearing on the other side. She immediately needed technological help to amplify her hearing. She managed the clinical settings well.

Robert M. Hensel says, 'I choose not to place "DIS" in my ability.' Sandy Fussell adds: 'Life is all about balance. Since I have only one leg, I understand that well.' We must all understand that hard things are put in our way, not to stop us but to invoke our

17. Lauren Love, 'Disabusing Disability: A Doctor's Paralyzing Injury Brings New Perspective' *Michigan Medicine* (2 February 2018), available at: https://www.michiganmedicine.org/health-lab/disabusing-disability-doctors-paralyzing-injury-brings-new-perspective (accessed 12 December 2024)

18. Docs with Disabilities Initiative (DwDI), available at: https://www.docswithdisabilities.org/ (accessed 11 December 2024)

courage and strength. Remember – keep your face always towards the sunshine. The shadows will fall behind you. Your success and happiness lie in you. Start doing what is necessary. Then, do what is possible. Soon, you will be doing the impossible. This is the joy of life.

Prof. Balram K. Gupta

Prof. (Dr.) Balram K. Gupta has had a distinguished career spanning over five decades, contributing significantly to legal education, legal practice, and judicial education. He served as Director of the National Judicial Academy, Bhopal (2013), and later as Director (Academics) at the Chandigarh Judicial Academy (2015). He has been both Professor Emeritus and Senior Advocate, excelling in academia and the legal profession. His academic journey includes working as a Young Social Scientist under Prof. J.A.G. Griffith at the London School of Economics (1978) and participating in the U.S. Government's International Visitors Programme (1988). He was the youngest Professor of Law and Chairman, Department of Laws, Panjab University (1986–1989), and later Honorary Dean, Faculty of Law, Guru Nanak Dev University. Transitioning to legal practice in 1991, he was designated a Senior Advocate at the Punjab & Haryana High Court. His contributions to legal and judicial education were recognised by Panjab University at its first Global Alumni Meet (2018).

A committed Rotarian since 1976, Dr. Gupta has integrated Rotary values with the judiciary through lectures, orations, and writings. Rotary International honoured him with the Lifetime Achievement Award in 2016. His autobiography – *My Journey with Law & Justice* (2022), written in a style akin to Lord Denning's, intertwines law with literature, preserving legal thought through literary expression. Hailed as the Indian counterpart to Lord Denning, he continues to shape contemporary legal discourse as a columnist for *The Indian Express* and *Lawyers Update*.

Disability Discrimination at the Workplace – A Case for Compassion

Bhagwan Dass v. Punjab State Electricity Board

Francisca Pretorius

When you focus on someone's disability, you'll overlook their abilities, beauty, and uniqueness. Once you learn to accept and love them for who they are, you subconsciously learn to love yourself unconditionally.

—Yvonne Pierre, *The Day My Soul Cried: A Memoir*

Disability and illness are intrinsic aspects of the human experience. How we care for those who are suffering from such maladies reveals our character as individuals and our compassion and humanity as a society. Anthropologist Margaret Mead was once asked about the first evidence of civilisation.[1] Her answer: a human thigh bone with a healed fracture found at an archaeological site dating back 15,000 years—not tools for hunting or religious artefacts. The

1. Ira Byock, *The Best Care Possible: A Physician's Quest to Transform Care Through the End of Life* (Avery, 2012)

healed bone signifies that someone cared for the injured individual long enough for the fracture to heal, providing shelter, protection, and sustenance. To Mead, these acts of care and compassion were the true signs of civilisation, allowing our species to thrive.

Most of us are likely to experience some form of short-term or long-term illness or disability at some point in our lives. Of course, the level of impairment varies greatly, depending on aspects such as age, sex, ethnicity, and economic status, as well as how a community supports or interacts with that disability. It is estimated that around 1.3 billion people, or a staggering 16% of the global population, live with significant disabilities.[2] In the United States, the Center for Disease Control and Prevention estimates that as many as one in four adults live with at least one disability.[3] It should come as no surprise that disability disproportionately affects those who are disadvantaged in other ways. For example, the World Bank estimates that more than 20% of the world's poorest people live with some kind of disability, and women with disabilities are at higher risk of experiencing harm or abuse.[4]

The United Nations Convention on the Rights of Persons with Disabilities (UNCRPD), ratified by over 180 states, mandates that nations ensure individuals with disabilities are afforded the full enjoyment of their human rights and receive equitable treatment under the law. Despite this global directive, Persons with Disabilities

---

2. World Health Organization, 'Disability and Health' (7 March 2023), available at: https://www.who.int/news-room/fact-sheets/detail/disability-and-health (accessed 20 July 2024)

3. Centers for Disease Control and Prevention, 'Disability Inclusion' (2020), available at: https://www.cdc.gov/ncbddd/disabilityandhealth/disability-inclusion.html (accessed 20 July 2024)

4. United Nations, 'Factsheet on Persons with Disabilities' (2021), available at: https://www.un.org/development/desa/disabilities/resources/factsheet-on-persons-with-disabilities.html (accessed 20 July 2024)

worldwide continue to be vulnerable and face considerable barriers in accessing justice, education, healthcare, and employment.[5] One significant impediment to meaningful progress within the disability sector is the deficiency of domestic legislation tailored to protect and empower disabled persons. Additionally, while the basic right to non-discrimination is enshrined in numerous modern constitutions, regrettably, the ideal of equality prescribed by law often fails to manifest.

Regarding employment discrimination against individuals with disabilities, out of the global working-age population of 5.12 billion,[6] an estimated 470 million have some form of disability.[7] Persons with Disabilities have notably lower employment rates compared to the general population, and this disparity has widened over the last few decades.[8] In some countries, the unemployment rate for Persons with Disabilities can reach up to 80%.[9] Stereotypes unjustly imply that having a disability reduces a person's aptitude to work effectively. While adjustments may often be necessary, redundancy is not.

Take India as an example. Of the 1.4 billion people in India, an estimated 40 to 90 million people have one or more disabilities. Of

---

5. Thomson Reuters Foundation, 'Empowering People with Disabilities: A Comparative Study of Disability Legislation' (17 June 2015), available at: https://www.trust.org/publications/i/?id=0f116ebd-2821-40df-95aa-daa1fa8eb681 (accessed 10 August 2024)

6. World Bank, 'Population ages 15-64, total' (2023), available at: https://data.worldbank.org/indicator/SP.POP.1564.TO (accessed 20 July 2024)

7. International Labour Organization, 'Facts on Disability in the World of Work' (2007), available at: https://www.ilo.org/sites/default/files/wcmsp5/groups/public/@dgreports/@dcomm/documents/publication/wcms_087707.pdf

8. World Health Organization, 'Disability' (7 March 2023), available at: https://www.who.int/news-room/fact-sheets/detail/disability-and-health (accessed 20 July 2024)

9. International Labour Organization, 'Disability and Work', available at: https://www.ilo.org/topics/disability-and-work (accessed 20 July 2024)

these, approximately 13 million are considered employable, but only about 3.4 million have secured employment in both the organised and unorganised sectors through government-led schemes or self-employment initiatives. Fortunately, India has enacted specific anti-discrimination and disability-focused legislation; however, the implementation of the legislation leaves much to be desired.

It is in this context that the case of *Bhagwan Dass and Another v. Punjab State Electricity Board*[10] is particularly edifying. This litigation spotlights the wrongful termination of an employee who became disabled during his tenure, probing the protections afforded under Indian disability laws and the lack of application. It underscores not only the ongoing challenges faced by Persons with Disabilities but also the judiciary's potential to affirm fundamental human rights and dignity. The case serves as a stark reminder of the need for heightened awareness and sensitivity towards disability, advocating for a more inclusive legal environment as well as compassionate social transformation and support structures where individuals with disabilities are not viewed as inferior but are recognised as a vital part of our community.

Factual Background

Many years ago, on 19 July 1977, Bhagwan Dass joined the Punjab State Electricity Board (PSEB or the Board) on an *ad hoc* basis. After four years of *ad hoc* work, Shri Dass was appointed as a full-time employee and promoted to the position of Assistant Lineman in 1981. Unfortunately, after almost 17 years of dedicated service, he suffered an episode of sudden visual impairment in January 1994 that eventually led to complete blindness. Consequently, he was absent from duty from the date of the ill-fated event. Due to his absence, the PSEB issued two memoranda in 1994, directing

10. (2008) 1 SCC 579

him to report back to duty, but he did not respond or comply, leading to a charge sheet being issued against him.

The matter remained dormant until July 1997, when Shri Dass, grappling with his blindness, informed the Board about his condition and requested voluntary retirement. Anticipating the loss of income as the provider of the household, he additionally asked for a suitable job for his wife. The Board, acknowledging his request, issued an order on 14 December 1999, retrospectively relieving Shri Dass from service effective 21 March 1997, the date when his medical certificate of blindness was issued. Furthermore, the chargesheet against him was withdrawn on 13 January 1999, and he was asked to submit a leave application for his period of absence.

Later, Shri Dass learned about his rights under the Persons with Disabilities (Equal Opportunities, Protection of Rights and Full Participation) Act of 1995 (PwD Act), which provides protection to employees who acquire disabilities during their service. Learning that he was not compelled to retire due to his blindness, he sought to withdraw his retirement request. Despite explaining his condition and citing his rights under the Act, the departmental authorities refused his request.

From the facts, it is evident that the Board was fully aware of the relevant circulars from the Punjab Government and the Board regarding the implementation of the PwD Act, which afforded Shri Dass certain rights and imposed specific obligations on the Board. Nevertheless, they denied him his rightful protection.

Faced with this injustice, Shri Dass, joined by his son, filed a civil writ petition in the Punjab and Haryana High Court. In this petition, they sought relief in terms of reinstatement under Section 47 of the PwD Act and the relevant circulars. Additionally, as an alternative relief, they requested employment for their son in his place. The High Court, however, focused primarily on the alternative relief of employment for Bhagwan Dass's son and dismissed the writ petition. The court's brief order did not mention Section 47 of the PwD Act or Shri Dass's rights under that provision. Dissatified with this decision, Bhagwan Dass and his son appealed to the Supreme Court.

Enshrined Rights

In its decision, the Supreme Court focused primarily on the 'clear and definite legislative mandate' of the PwD Act. Under Section 47 of the Act, the rights of an employee who develops a disability during service are protected and safeguarded. The Act mandates that no employee who develops a disability during their service can be dismissed or demoted based solely on their disability. An employee experiencing disability must be deemed in service and entitled to all service benefits, including annual increments and promotions, until the day of retirement. If an employee can no longer perform their original duties due to their disability, the law requires that they be reassigned to a suitable post with the same pay-scale and service benefits. If reassignment is not possible, the employee should be placed in a supernumerary post until a suitable position is available or until they reach superannuation. Additionally, the law explicitly states that an employee's promotion cannot be denied merely because of their disability, ensuring that their career progression remains unaffected by their change in physical capabilities.

While the Constitution of India provides protection for Persons with Disabilities, the Supreme Court's decision to emphasise legislative protections under the PwD Act rather than invoking constitutional provisions directly does not exclude the underlying constitutional principles of equality and non-discrimination, which implicitly underpin the legislative framework.

Ruling: Legality, as well as Character and Humanity

The bench comprising Justice Aftab Alam and Justice G.P. Mathur delivered a scathing judgment, underscoring not only the statutory obligations but also the moral responsibilities owed to employees who become disabled during their tenure.

The court, in the judgment authored by Justice Alam, held that the Board wrongfully and illegally terminated Shri Dass and that he should have been protected under the PwD Act. The court ruled that Shri Dass must be considered continuously employed from the time of his alleged termination until his legal retirement age, holding that he was entitled to receive all standard employment benefits, including annual increments and any due promotions, from 1997 until his retirement. Any terminal benefits that were paid to him prematurely were directed to be recalculated and credited against the wages he should have earned during this period. If there was any excess amount after this adjustment, it was ordered that it should be returned to him in manageable monthly instalments from his future salary. The court ruled that Shri Dass had to be officially reinstated and had to receive all owed payments, adjusted as specified, within six weeks from the date of the judgment.

Furthermore, the Supreme Court of India criticised the Board for its lack of sensitivity and for violating the explicit protections afforded by the law. The court pointed out that the Board's actions reflected a deep-seated insensitivity and a misunderstanding of the spirit of the law designed to protect and empower Persons with Disabilities. The court noted that the Board had acted in a manner that was both legally incorrect and morally reprehensible by choosing to interpret Shri Dass's request for retirement—a request made without full awareness of his rights—as voluntary, thereby denying him the protections he was entitled to under the law. The judgment emphasised that the actions of the Board's officers demonstrated a lack of empathy and character and lamented that such attitudes towards disabled employees perpetuate discrimination and social exclusion, contrary to the objectives of the PwD Act.

Lack of Societal Support Structures and Delayed Justice

The case of Shri Dass poignantly illustrates the profound delays and challenges faced from the onset of his disability in 1994 to the Supreme Court's judgment in 2008. This prolonged legal battle underscores not only the offical inefficiencies but also the broader societal failures in providing adequate support systems for Persons with Disabilities. Between 1994, when his disability first manifested, and 2000, when he finally took legal action, Shri Dass undoubtedly endured significant adversity without sufficient institutional support. This time likely marked a period of intense uncertainty and hardship, worsened by his new disability, loss of income, and a lack of effective advocacy or assistance. The case then took another eight years to reach a resolution, demonstrating the need for enhanced support mechanisms to not only improve legal responses but also bolster societal infrastructure to better support individuals with disabilities.

New Legislation in India, but Continued Lack of Support Structures

Following India's ratification of the UNCRPD in 2007, efforts to overhaul the existing PwD Act of 1995 commenced in 2010.[11] This was aimed at aligning the national legislation with the

11. C.L. Narayan and T. John, 'The Rights of Persons with Disabilities Act, 2016: Does it Address the Needs of the Persons with Mental Illness and Their Families' (2017) 59(1) *Indian J Psychiatry* 17, DOI: 10.4103/psychiatry.IndianJPsychiatry_75_17

international standards set by the UNCRPD. The new Rights of Persons with Disabilities Act was developed and subsequently passed by both houses of the Parliament in 2016. Various changes were introduced to ensure compliance with UNCRPD, and the scope of protection for Persons with Disabilities was widened significantly.[12] Despite the enhanced safeguards, its practical application has encountered considerable obstacles, as highlighted by the Supreme Court in the case of *Seema Girija Lal v. Union of India.*[13] The initial court directive in January 2023 revealed significant non-compliance across various states, leading to further directives from the Supreme Court urging the department dealing with the subject of disabilities to improve coordination with state governments to enforce the Act effectively. More than seven years after the new legislation's enactment, thirteen states still had not appointed state disability commissioners, sixteen had not designated special public prosecutors, and four were without any established special courts.[14] This situation underscores a broader lack of societal support structures that are crucial for upholding the rights of Persons with Disabilities, reflecting systemic neglect in the provision of not only necessary legal and administrative frameworks but also societal and community care.

---

12. Herbert Smith Freehills, 'Implementation of the Rights of Persons with Disabilities Act, 2016' (26 October 2017), *available at:* https://www.herbertsmithfreehills.com/notes/employment/2017-10/india-implementation-of-the-rights-of-persons-with-disabilities-act-2016 (accessed 10 August 2024)

13. 2023 SCC OnLine SC 854

14. Sushovan Patnaik, 'On Disability Rights, We Need to Look Beyond the Supreme Court' *SCO* (19 November 2023), available at: https://www.scobserver.in/journal/on-disability-rights-we-need-to-look-beyond-the-supreme-court/ (accessed 10 August 2024)

Comparative Example: United States of America

In the United States, the Americans with Disabilities Act (ADA), 1990 forbids discrimination against individuals based on their disability. This legislation supports disability inclusion across various areas of life by empowering Persons with Disabilities to address discrimination in employment, public services, and public accommodations. The primary aim of the ADA is to ensure equal opportunity, encourage full participation, enable independent living, and foster economic self-sufficiency for Americans with disabilities. Despite this law being in full force and effect for many decades, blatant forms of discrimination against Persons with Disabilities are still being heard to this day.

In a notable case[15] adjudicated by the U.S. Equal Employment Opportunity Commission (EEOC), a jury awarded $1.675 million to a deaf Applicant who was discriminated against by McLane Northeast, a distribution company in New York.[16] The case revolved around the company's refusal to interview and subsequently hire the deaf candidate for two warehouse positions after learning of her disability. The trial, which lasted three and a half days, concluded with the jury deliberating for only two hours before reaching their decision. The damages awarded included $25,000 for back pay, $150,000 for emotional distress, and $1.5 million in punitive damages, reflecting a strong stance against disability discrimination and underscoring the protections afforded under the ADA.

---

15. *United States Equal Emp't Opportunity Comm'n v. Mclane/Eastern, Inc.*, 5:20-cv-1628 (BKS/ML) N.D.N.Y., (23 August 2023)

16. Equal Employment Opportunity Commission Press Release, 'Jury Awards $1.675 Million in EEOC Disability Discrimination Case Against McLane Northeast' (2 August 2024), available at: https://www.eeoc.gov/newsroom/jury-awards-1675-million-eeoc-disability-discrimination-case-against-mclane-northeast (accessed 10 August 2024)

Similar to the *Bhagwan Dass* case, the law was clear, and the company acted illegally. Moreover, the hiring team made a deliberate decision not to interview and hire a deaf candidate after learning of her disability. The profound insensitivity and lack of compassion of the individuals involved in the hiring decision gave rise to the large punitive award against the company.

Conclusion

While court decisions, such as the *Bhagwan Dass* case, and legislation have improved in recent years, we need more than a legal shift to end the discrimination against Persons with Disabilities. We need a societal shift towards compassion and humanity, where we do not regard Persons with Disabilities as 'less than' but rather as an important and intrinsic part of the fabric of society, where they are celebrated and not discarded. Until such a societal shift occurs, legislation and regulatory frameworks designed to protect individuals with disabilities will remain inadequate, failing to fully address the needs and rights of this important minority group.

As an added benefit, this mindset shift would not only improve the lives of those living with disabilities but of everyone. This is brilliantly illustrated by the so-called curb-cut effect.[17] In the 1960s, the Curb Cut movement emerged in California, led by Ed Roberts, a graduate student at the University of California, Berkeley, who was paralysed due to polio. Determined to study and advocate for disability rights, Roberts catalysed a significant movement alongside other disabled students, pushing for inclusivity and accessibility in public spaces. The movement led to the implementation of Berkeley's pioneering Curb Cut

17. Angela Glover Blackwell, 'The Curb Cut Effect' *Stanford Social Innovation Review* (2017), available at: https://ssir.org/articles/entry/the_curb_cut_effect# (accessed 10 August 2024)

programme in 1971 and also exemplified the 'curb cut effect', illustrating that designs accommodating disabilities often benefit everyone. For instance, curb cuts designed for wheelchair access also aid people with babies in strollers, the elderly using walkers, and travellers with suitcases. These innovations underscored the broader benefits of inclusive design. This proactive stance on accessibility eventually influenced legislative changes, culminating in the ADA mentioned above.

Working towards such a compassion-driven societal shift is vital to nurturing an inclusive and fair space for people living with disabilities, where their rights are not merely inscribed in legal texts but are fully experienced in their everyday lives.

Francisca Pretorius

Francisca Pretorius is an international lawyer and formerly the Adviser and Head of the Office of Civil and Criminal Justice Reform at the Commonwealth Secretariat, London.

She has played a major role in the Commonwealth Secretariat's Military Justice Transformation project, assisting member nations in initiating reforms in their systems of military justice.

She has had a varied international career spanning corporate law in South Africa and the United States, as well as lecturing in South Africa and Kenya.

Licensed to practice law in South Africa and the US, Francisca merges legal expertise with a global perspective, advocating for justice and sustainability.

She holds an LLB, an LLM in International Trade Law, and an MBA in Global, Social, and Sustainable Enterprise.

Inaugurating a Discourse of Autonomy and Choice

Suchita Srivastava v. Chandigarh Administration

Prof. Amita Dhanda

Introduction

The fatigue of being seen with the eyes of another or not being seen at all was amongst the motivations for persons with disabilities to demand a United Nations Convention on the Rights of Persons with Disabilities. The slogan of "Nothing About Us Without Us" resonated in the hall housing the Ad Hoc Committee deliberating on the Convention where persons with disabilities sparred with the non-disabled to be seen as they saw themselves and not how the non-disabled world chose to see them. The deliberations were contentious on several issues but the longest dragging of feet occurred around the recognition of full legal capacity for all persons with disabilities in all aspects of life. State parties were agreeable to recognise legal capacity but not for all persons with disabilities. They insisted upon an exception for persons intellectual, psychosocial and developmental disabilities. After many skirmishes and some dissimulations, which are not the concern of this article[1], Article12 of the United Nations Convention on the Rights of Persons with Disabilities (hereinafter UNCRPD) was adopted recognizing the legal capacity of all persons with disabilities in all aspects of life on an equal basis with others.

India signed the UNCRPD in March 2007 and ratified it in October 2007 so when the Convention came into force in May 2008, India was amongst the countries who had bound themselves to implement the Convention. The statute to enforce the Convention was only enacted in 2016, but the CRPD became relevant for India even before the enactment because Indian jurisprudence allows for the direct enforcement of international human rights even before it is expressly incorporated in municipal law. Moreover, the Indian Constitution requires the Indian State to undertake its activities duly respecting international law. The case, *Suchita Srivastava and Another v. Chandigarh Administration,*[2] which is the focus of this comment was adjudicated upon before the UNCRPD was incorporated in domestic law. The Convention was expressly referred to in the apex court and point of controversy in the case has been expressly addressed by the UNCRPD. The final decision of the Supreme Court of India can be claimed to be in conformity with the CRPD, though the reasons provided for the decision swing between the zones of choice and protection. This matter of a young woman with intellectual disability who wished to retain her foetus came in appeal to the Supreme Court against a ruling of the division bench of the Punjab and Haryana High Court which did not agree with the opinion of a medical board and ordered the pregnancy of a young woman with

1. For an analytical narrative on the travails of inducting legal capacity in the CRPD, see Amita Dhanda, "Legal Capacity in the Disability rights Convention: Stranglehold of the Past or Lodestar for the Future" (2006-2007) 34 *Syracuse Journal of International Law and Commerce* 429-461

2. (2009) 9 SCC 1

intellectual disability to be terminated because in the court's view she lacked the intellectual, social and economic resources to bring up the child when born.

The termination, the High Court held, was required for both the welfare of the pregnant woman and the prospective child. The decision pronounced by the High Court, though not in conformity with how disabled people view the matter of their will and preference, was representative of the way in which persons with disabilities and their preferences have been long viewed by the non-disabled world.

The Supreme Court reversed the decision of the High Court, despite the reversal, it has been asked by others[3] and me[4] whether the court in reaching the decision was guided by the disability rights jurisprudence of the UNCRPD? Or can the ruling be seen to exemplify the charge that Ratna Kapur makes with regard to several pro-women decisions of the Supreme Court, that they were poorly reasoned even if correct decisions[5].

Instead of repeating the critique I revisit *Suchita Srivastava*[6] to ask whether the correctness of the decision and its real-time consequences[7] can be built upon to create an emancipatory

3. Archana Parashar, "Right to have Rights - Supreme Court as the Guarantor of the Rights of Persons with Mental Intellectual Disability" (2011-12) 5 *Indian Journal of Constitutional Law* 160

4. Amita Dhanda, "The Disability Weave of the Indian Supreme Court- the First 75 Years" in *Justice for the Nation* (Thomson Reuters, 2024)

5. Ratna Kapur and Brenda, Cossman *Subversive Sites: Feminist Engagements with Law in India* (1996)

6. *Supra* note 2

7. The protagonist is working as an attendant in the same institution in which she was living and has acquired the reputation of being an amazing cook. Her daughter lived with her till class VIII but now is studying in a boarding school in the city. Personal Communication received on 25th April 2024 from Tanu Bedi one of the advocates in *Suchita*

discourse for women with disabilities in India. The judgment rewriting project has demonstrated that often scholastic initiative can complete what judicial reasoning had left unfinished. This article is not an effort to rewrite *Suchita*, rather it aims to look at the expressed preference of the appellant in the light of a decisions like *Vali*[8] where the testimony of a blind woman has not been evaluated on benchmarks relevant for a sighted person. A blind woman the court points out relies upon hearing and not sight to recognise people. Her voice recognition capacities cannot be treated at par with a sighted person.

I am revisiting *Suchita* not only to point out what it failed to do but to also acknowledge what it did and contend that even if incompletely, *Suchita* initiated the discourse of autonomy and choice for persons with intellectual disabilities. To undertake this exercise, I firstly recount the decisions of the High Court and Supreme Court, I next compare the two decisions and tease out the pro-disability statements in the Supreme Court's judgment. Lastly, I reflect on the missing pieces in the Supreme Court's pronouncement which need to be incrementally supplied in the jurisprudence evolving after Suchita.

No Right to Parenthood – The Decision of the High Court

An orphan woman with intellectual disability living in a woman protective home was repeatedly raped by more than one security guard. She was transferred to another home where it was discovered that she was pregnant.[9] The administrators of the home

8. *Patan Jamal Vali v. State of Andhra Pradesh* (hereinafter *Vali*), (2021) 16 SCC 225

9. Since the woman was also a rape victim both the High Court and the Supreme Court have not named her but only referred to her as the victim in their orders. Since this case is more about her agency than her exploitation, I agree with Archana Parashar that it is important to embody her and not to reinforce her

constituted a multi-member medical board who advised medical termination of the pregnancy as the Board was of the view that the protagonist despite her assertions to the contrary was not in a position to bring up the child on her own. The plea of an orphan to have someone in the world who would be her own was considered immature and irrational. In the face of the protagonist's persistent refusal to undergo the abortion, the Chandigarh Administration moved the High Court seeking permission to go ahead with the abortion without her consent even though Section 3(4) of the Medical Termination of Pregnancy Act, 1971 prohibited a medical termination of pregnancy without the consent of the woman.[10]

In its preliminary order the High Court was of the view that it needed to determine whether the matter should be decided in terms of the statutory provision or by drawing upon the *parens patriae* power of the court? In order to take an error free decision, the court constituted a second Medical Board and asked it to provide its opinion on the 13 issues formulated by the court. The court's views could be deduced from the following directive where it stated:

> If the Expert Body forms a bona-fide opinion that the pregnancy needs to be medically terminated in the best interest of the victim, we in exercise of our *parens patriae* jurisdiction, direct the petitioner Administration to admit the victim in the Government Medical College and Hospital, Sector 32, Chandigarh, constitute a team of Medical Experts comprising not less than two Gynaecologists and the other

---

victimhood. To protect her privacy and yet not reinforce her victimhood I have unlike Parashar not used her name but referred to her as the protagonist

10. *Chandigarh Administration v. Nemo,* CWP no. 8760 of 2009, order dated 17 July 2009, *available at:* https://indiankanoon.org/doc/1067943/ (accessed 12 October 2024)

> related associates, who shall then terminate the pregnancy of the victim forthwith and without any delay as soon as the report of the Expert Body is received.[11]

Despite the directions given by the court, the medical board felt unable to go ahead with the abortion and the reports of the various experts were submitted before the court to take the final call. The court then goes through the various reports, according greater weightage to reports which counselled termination[12] over the ones which asked the court to respect the protagonist's will and preference.[13]

Legal, social, and psychological arguments were pressed before the Punjab and Haryana High Court to respect the protagonist's choice. The court however, after considering the physical conditions, mental capacity, social environment, and social support available to the mother, in the exercise of its *parens patriae* power decided that in the best interests of the foetus and the protagonist that the pregnancy be terminated.

On the question of the protagonist's preference, the court observed:

---

11. *Chandigarh Administration v. Nemo,* CWP no. 8760 of 2009, order dated 9 July 2009, *available at:* https://indiankanoon.org/doc/622591/ (accessed 12 October 2024). There were other directions in the order on the quality of care to be provided to the protagonist and preserving the foetus for the impending criminal trial, which are not of relevance to this article

12. Since the protagonist is a person with mental retardation the report of the psychiatrist is described to be "of immense value and crucial for the formation of a final view in the matter". The court considers it appropriate to reproduce this report in extenso in the judgment, *supra* note 10, para 10

13. Whilst expressing its impatience with the Expert Body at failing to act in the matter the court points out how "the learned Judicial Officer, while compiling the opinion of the subject-experts, has also loaded the report with her own opinion against termination of the pregnancy". *Id.,* para 9

> What she has consented for is something which she has absolutely no knowledge of. In our view, the victim cannot be said to have consented for retention of the pregnancy caused by the brutal act of rape for the obvious reason that she does not know as to how conception takes place.[14]

And reiterating what the court saw as its *parens patriae* obligation, the court asked:

> Would it not be mere poetic justice if we, notwithstanding our profound belief, are swayed by the emotional hue and cry made on behalf of a physically grown but mentally weak person who does not understand the consequences of what she is asking for, and allow that unborn child to enter this world even with the possible risk of physical deformities and an inadequate mother, or should we allow the victim to liberate herself from the forced physical, mental, moral and social responsibility which she is neither capable of shouldering nor aware of as to how has she been burdened with it?[15]

The High Court, relying on the views of expert bodies and medical assessments, directed the termination of the pregnancy. By the time these deliberations concluded, the pregnancy had progressed to a stage where medical risks were a growing concern.[16] The court, however, focused on the expert recommendations before

---

14. *Id.*, para 32

15. *Id.*, para 29

16. For a biological parent the impact of the procedure on the life and health of the woman assumes critical importance. In *A (mother of X) v. State of Maharashtra,* 2024 INSC 371 the delayed discovery of the pregnancy of a sexually assaulted teenage daughter caused a mother to decide against abortion because it could endanger the life and health of the daughter

it and issued its directive without prolonged engagement with the surrounding circumstances. It was this order that was subsequently challenged before the Supreme Court through an urgent appeal for reconsideration.

Not Without Her Consent, Says the Supreme Court

The appeal to the Supreme Court was prompted by concerns that the High Court's decision did not sufficiently engage with the individual's personal views and preferences in the matter. The apex court was required to consider whether a pregnancy could be medically terminated without the consent of the woman? And could the court in exercise of its *parens patriae* power order such termination for a woman with intellectual disability?

In responding to these questions, the court firstly emphasised how an abortion could not take place without the consent of the woman. The requirement has been expressly incorporated in the MTP Act. Furthermore "a woman's right to make reproductive choices is also a dimension of `personal liberty' as understood under Article 21 of the Constitution of India. It is important to recognise that reproductive choices can be exercised to procreate as well as to abstain from procreating. The crucial consideration is that a woman›s right to privacy, dignity and bodily integrity should be respected."[17]

The MTP Act makes an exception in relation to minors and women with mental illness where the consent of the guardian has been considered as statutorily sufficient. Since the protagonist was an orphan could the court decide on her behalf? The Supreme Court relying on a range of reasons answered in the negative.

The court began its reasoning by firstly referring to the text of the MTP Act and pointed to the fact that the statute does not

17. *Supra* note 2, para 22

mention women with mental retardation amongst the category of women whose guardians could provide consent on their behalf. Only minors and women with mental illness were so mentioned. It can be said that the court in making this analysis literally interpreted the relevant provision and presumed that non-inclusion of mental retardation was considered and deliberate.[18] The court refers to India's ratification of the UNCRPD but does not ask whether the systems of substituted decision-making would survive for any disability be it psycho-social or intellectual? Since courts do not answer academic questions and the case before the court concerned a woman with intellectual disability, the court limited its decision to her and ruled that the system of substituted decision-making had not been put in place for a 'woman with mental retardation'.

While addressing the question of the *parens patriae* power, the court differentiated between various degrees of mental retardation, and categorized the protagonist as a case of mild or borderline retardation who could carry out the activities of daily survival. In the face of this functional capability, the court did not think that ordering an abortion against her will at such an advanced stage of pregnancy was in her best interest. Moreover, in light of the principles embodied in the CRPD, the importance of recognising and respecting the autonomy and decision-making of Persons with Disabilities, including women, was an underlying consideration. The court's conclusion that abortion was not in the best interest of the protagonist was reached after taking note of her functional abilities, advanced pregnancy, expressed preference and the CRPD. The reasoning is not clear on the weightage given to each factor.

---

18. It is possible to argue that the court looked at the segregation of mental illness and mental retardation in a facile manner due to the definition of mentally ill person in the Mental Health Act of 1987. Whether a definition of a care and treatment statute should be extended to the MTP Act was not examined by the court

Even so the court did not brush away her choice and did not let her disability totally negate her capabilities. It did not rule that persons with intellectual disability had full legal capacity on an equal basis with others. Nor did it say that persons with mental retardation inherently lacked the capacity to decide for themselves. Instead, it asked whether this person with mental retardation lacked the capacity to exercise her reproductive choice? And found her capable.

Archana Parashar in her comment on the case saw the judgment of the Supreme Court as a lost opportunity.[19] The court, she opined needed to grapple with the connection between disability, legal capacity and the consequential impact of this connection to the rights of persons with disabilities. The court's failure to address this foundational issue and thereby adopt a principled position in the matter is Parashar's dissatisfaction with the judgment. The court may have provided relief, but it has not created jurisprudence which could be drawn upon in like cases. Even as I agree with Parashar's analysis I suggest that we must also look at some of the pro-autonomy and choice seeds sown in *Suchita* which have been nourished by subsequent case law. And it is useful to look at Parashar's analysis to understand why the court has struggled when faced with difficult questions of reproductive choice.

Jurisprudence of Reproductive Rights: After *Suchita*

The protagonist of *Suchita* was an unmarried woman with intellectual disability who became pregnant after being raped and yet wanted to continue her pregnancy. She was running afoul of many popular moral registers. The High Court decision speaks of her wanting to continue her pregnancy because she did not make the connection between the sexual assault and the pregnancy. She did not know of the moral opprobrium that she would receive by

19. *Supra* note 3

reason of being an unwed mother. However, this young woman was persistent in expressing her choice and that expression caused the medical board to opine that the termination could not be ordered without her consent. The High Court's approach may have been shaped by the limited nature of its engagement with the individual, as its assessment was based on reports rather than a direct interaction. Nevertheless, when the matter reached the Supreme Court, the bench took a broader view of her circumstances and granted the relief she was seeking, offering a resolution that aligned more closely with her expressed wishes.

In *Patan Jamal Vali v. State of Andhra Pradesh*[20] the Supreme Court accorded credence to the testimony of a blind woman because as a blind woman her auditory recognition was better developed than a sighted person. In providing this reason for according probity to Vali's testimony, the court moved away from the deficits understanding of disability and asked for disability to be seen as difference. I see an early effort being made in *Suchita* when the court questioned the lumping of all women with intellectual disability. Unlike *Vali*, the *Suchita* court did not look at the protagonist's preference as a preference of an orphan with disability. Even as the *Vali* reasoning can better explain why the preference of the woman with disability should be deferred to.

In *Suchita* the Supreme Court spoke of a woman's bodily integrity and her autonomy to decide whether to continue or terminate her pregnancy. Unlike the High Court, the apex court in *Suchita* accorded no importance to the marital status of the woman in respecting her preference to continue her pregnancy. In *X v. Principal Secretary Health and Family Welfare*[21] the choice

20. *Supra* note 8

21. SLP (Civil) no. 12612 of 2022, *available at:* https://indiankanoon.org/doc/134729746/ (accessed 15 October 2024)

of a woman to terminate her pregnancy has been delinked from her marital status. A logical progression from *Suchita.* However, as pointed out by Parashar, since *Suchita* attempted to resolve the question of reproductive choice without asking the hard questions around the attribution of incapacity to persons with disabilities, the court has not been able to build on the pro-choice decisions it has made. If termination of pregnancy is permitted to save the life or protect the health of the woman, then is such protection limited to physical health? If not, then how can the court justify its refusal to permit a woman afflicted with post-partum psychosis to terminate her pregnancy after the duration permitted by law had expired.[22] The subtext of *Suchita* was that considering her joyful expectation of the impending birth, the protagonist should be allowed to continue her pregnancy. Would the same reasoning not apply to fears of doom?

Conclusion

Suchita Srivastava was a landmark decision which inaugurated the discourse of autonomy and choice even if it did not confront the many difficult questions surrounding the deprivation of legal capacity of persons with disabilities. Since it chose correctly, I suggest that judicial pronouncements that follow *Suchita* as well as academic writing elaborating on the decision should untangle its many confusions and replace its inarticulate preferences with reasoned elaboration. The task of reflecting on difficult questions of life and law need not be only performed by the court before whom they are first raised. Rather inspiration should be taken by judges and jurists from the incremental approach of common law.

---

22. *X v. Union of India,* 2023 INSC 919

Prof. Amita Dhanda

Dr. Amita Dhanda is Professor-Emerita at the National Academy of Legal Studies and Research, Hyderabad, where she also heads the Centre for Disability Studies. Dr. Dhanda has been working in the field of disability rights for more than 40 years. She was actively involved in formulating the first and the latest disability statutes in the country. Her expertise was employed by the Supreme Court of India to examine the plight of persons with mental illness in the jails of West Bengal. The investigation resulted in the Supreme Court declaring the housing of mentally ill persons in jails to be unconstitutional. More recently, the Supreme Court has asked the Centre for Disability Studies to examine and report on the status of the right to accessibility in the country. And the Report entitled "Finding Sizes for All" is under active consideration by the Supreme Court.

A comprehensive examination of the legal status of persons with mental illness in Indian Law resulted in her pioneering publication entitled *Legal Order and Mental Disorder* (Sage 2000), wherein she found that the denial of legal capacity to persons with mental illness substantially reinforced the social stigma experienced by the community. This insight from her doctoral work she employed to lobby for universal legal capacity with support in the United Nations Ad Hoc Committee on the Disability Rights Convention as a member of the World Network of Users and Survivors of Psychiatry (WNUSP). Subsequent to the adoption of the Convention on the Rights of Persons with Disabilities, she has been actively engaged in law reform activities in India along with providing consultative support to other countries. Dr. Dhanda is an international expert in the field of disability human rights, whereby she has not just argued for the human rights claims of Persons with Disabilities but also demonstrated how disability human rights would strengthen the human rights of all.

A Supreme Court Ruling that Gave Wings to the Disabled

Jeeja Ghosh v. Union of India

Manraj Grewal Sharma

Every day, the Punjab Governor and UT (Union Territory) administrator Banwari Lal Purohit receives one email from a parent of a disabled person, seeking some basic convenience for the group home for the disabled at Chandigarh. The parents, many of whom are distinguished residents of the city, have discovered the hard way that it's not easy to be heard when it comes to securing the rights for their wards with special needs, that it almost always requires a daily push to be heard. They know that one letter, even if signed by a legion of parents, including some very well-connected ones, will not move the needle. So, they have been writing an email every day since 2022. Justice does not come easily to the disabled. That is why the Supreme Court ruling in the *Jeeja Ghosh & ADAPT (Able Disabled All People Together) v. Union of India and Others*[1] (hereinafter *Jeeja Ghosh*) continues to be a landmark in this community's quest for an ordinary life. The ruling passed

1. (2016) 7 SCC 761

in May 2016 by the Supreme Court bench of Justice A.K. Sikri and Justice R.K. Agrawal led to significant reforms in the Civil Aviation Requirements (CAR), 2008, to ensure that Persons with Disabilities could fly with dignity.

Stella Young, the late Australian disability activist, who was also an acclaimed comedian and journalist, hit the nail on the head when she said, 'We're more disabled by the society that we live in than by our bodies and diagnoses.'[2] Jeeja Ghosh, a bubbly disability activist whose mere presence can lighten up a room, experienced this firsthand when she was flying to Goa to attend an international conference hosted by ADAPT (Able Disabled All People Together) on 19 February 2012. Jeeja was tightening her seat belt aboard a SpiceJet plane in Kolkata when a cabin crew told her that she was being deboarded because the captain was not comfortable with the idea of flying her. In tears, Ghosh protested vehemently but in vain and was forcibly taken off the plane and left at the airport. The feisty activist complained to the Ministry of Social Justice and Empowerment as well as to the Commissioner for Persons with Disabilities, West Bengal, and the Chief Commissioner for Persons with Disabilities, Government of India, which issued a notice to the airlines. SpiceJet responded by offering her a refund minus ₹1,500 as a cancellation fee. Later, Ghosh said it was like sprinkling salt on her wounds.

Upon enquiring from others in the community, she found that such maltreatment of the disabled was endemic to the aviation sector. Tony Kurian was repeatedly denied the right to purchase tickets on an Indigo flight because he was visually impaired. Nilesh Singit was told by a SpiceJet captain that he could not fly with

---

2. Corinna Bevier, 'Stella Young: "I'm Not Your Inspiration, Thank You Very Much."' (*The Student Movement, 3* January 2024), available at: https://www.andrews.edu/life/student-movement/issues/2024-03-01/a-e__stella-young.html (accessed 6 July 2024)

his crutches. Anilee Agarwal was forced to sign an indemnity bond before she could fly from Delhi to Raipur on Jet Connect, threatened with being 'body-lifted' by four male flight crew members, and finally 'thrown down the steps' in an aisle chair when she refused to be carried by hand.[3] Many disabled people had to sign indemnity bonds to board a plane. In short, flying was an invitation to a nightmare for most disabled persons.

The Legal Battle

Determined to ensure that things were set right for the community, Jeeja Ghosh filed a Public Interest Litigation (PIL) along with ADAPT in 2012, thus setting the stage for a critical examination of the Rights of Persons with Disabilities in India. The case challenged the discriminatory practices against disabled persons in the aviation sector, highlighting the violations of the Civil Aviation Requirements (CAR) of 2008. These regulations protect the rights and dignity of Persons with Disabilities and reduced mobility, in line with the United Nations Convention on the Rights of Persons with Disabilities (UNCRPD). These regulations mandate that airlines cannot refuse carriage to Persons with Disabilities and must provide necessary assistance without additional costs.

Ghosh and others submitted that the Union of India has an obligation to ensure that its citizens are not subject to such arbitrary and humiliating discrimination. It is a violation of their fundamental rights, including the right to life, the right to equality, the right to move freely throughout the territory of India, and the right to practice their profession. The State has an obligation to ensure these rights are protected—particularly for those who are disabled. More specifically, the Persons with Disabilities (Equal Opportunities, Protection of Rights and Full Participation) Act,

3. *Supra* note 1, para 15

1995 (Act, 1995) encapsulates the Government's obligations to ensure that those with disabilities can achieve their full potential free from such discrimination and harassment. The Act specifically deals with transportation systems, including airports and aircraft.

While SpiceJet responded quite negatively and tried to put the blame on Ghosh, claiming blood and froth were oozing out of her mouth – a charge backed by zero evidence – the Union Ministry of Aviation took it in the right spirit. As the ruling observed, the authorities did not treat the present petition as adversarial and accepted that such causes require a 'social context adjudication' approach.[4] To this end in mind, the Ministry of Civil Aviation appointed an expert committee known as the 'Ashok Kumar Committee' under the Chairmanship of G. Ashok Kumar, Joint Secretary, Aviation, to review the existing civil aviation rules regarding the disabled.

A Blueprint for Change

The Ashok Kumar Committee made several vital recommendations, including the standardisation of assistive devices, the establishment of dedicated help desks, and the proper training of airline and airport staff to handle disabled passengers sensitively. The Supreme Court directed the Directorate General of Civil Aviation (DGCA) to reconsider and incorporate the Committee's recommendations into the CAR, 2014. The critical recommendations included:

1. Standardisation of Assistive Devices: All airports should procure assistive equipment based on a standardised schedule in consultation with the Department of Disability Affairs. This ensures that all necessary devices are available and in good condition.

4. *Id.*, para 19

2. Dedicated Help Desks: Establishing fully accessible telephonic help desks to receive assistance requests from disabled passengers, ensuring their needs are communicated and met efficiently.

3. Training for Airline and Airport Staff: Comprehensive training programs for staff to develop awareness and sensitivity towards disabled passengers, ensuring they receive appropriate assistance and respect.

4. Accessible Infrastructure: Ensuring that airport facilities, including seating areas and restrooms, are designed to accommodate disabled passengers comfortably and safely.[5]

A Glimpse into the Ruling

Justice A.K. Sikri and Justice R.K. Agrawal, who authored the judgment, poignantly framed the issue by referencing Joseph P. Shapiro's book *No Pity*.[6] The Bench noted that societal ignorance and misunderstanding about the lives of disabled individuals set the tone for a judgment that critiques systemic failures and societal attitudes. The judgment acknowledged the strides made in recognising the rights of disabled persons through legislation and schemes, but pointed out the persistent gap between these laws and their implementation.

The Bench ruled that the subject of the Rights of Persons with Disabilities should be approached from a human rights perspective, which recognised that Persons with Disabilities were entitled to enjoy the full range of internationally guaranteed rights and freedoms without discrimination on the ground of disability. This creates an obligation on the part of the State to take positive

---

5. *Id.*, para 25

6. *Id.*, paras 1, 44

measures to ensure that Persons with Disabilities are enabled to exercise those rights. The Bench held that Jeeja Ghosh:

> was not given appropriate, fair, and caring treatment, which she required with due sensitivity, and the decision to de-board her, in the given circumstances, was uncalled for. More than that, the manner in which she was treated while de-boarding from the aircraft depicts a total lack of sensitivity on the part of the officials of the airlines. The manner in which she was dealt with proves the assertion of Shapiro as correct and justified that 'non-disabled do not understand disabled ones'.[7]

The judgment noted how SpiceJet's subsequent apology was inadequate as it trivialised the severity of the incident by merely referring to it as an 'inconvenience.'[8] The court ruled that the airlines had violated 1937 Rules and 2008 CAR guidelines, resulting in mental and physical suffering experienced by Jeeja Ghosh and unreasonable discrimination against her, and awarded her a sum of ₹10,00,000 as damages.[9]

The Broader Implications

The court's decision extended beyond Ghosh's case, addressing the broader issues faced by the disabled community. The judgment highlighted the necessity for systemic changes to ensure that disabled individuals can travel and live with dignity. The judgment delved into the legal framework governing the Rights of Persons with Disabilities in India, particularly CAR of 2008, whose provisions were violated by SpiceJet. The court also referenced international Conventions,

7. *Id.*, para 35

8. *Id.*, para 8

9. *Id.*, para 48

including the United Nations Convention on the Rights of Persons with Disabilities (UNCRPD), to which India is a signatory. The ruling noted, 'In international human rights law, equality is founded upon two complementary principles: non-discrimination and reasonable differentiation.'[10] It further held that disabled persons are viewed as abnormal, deserving of pity, and not as individuals entitled to the same opportunities as other members of society. This results in their 'exclusion both from the mainstream of the society and enjoyment of their fundamental rights and freedoms.'[11]

The court noted further:

> Persons with Disability are the most neglected lot not only in society but also in the family. More often, they are an object of pity. There are hardly any meaningful attempts to assimilate them into the mainstream of the nation's life. The apathy towards their problems is so pervasive that even the number of disabled persons existing in the country is not well documented.[12]

The court directed the DGCA and the Department of Disability Affairs to work together to fully implement the Ashok Kumar Committee's recommendations. This collaboration is crucial to ensuring that the rights of disabled passengers are upheld not just in letter but in spirit.[13]

A Landmark Win for Disability Rights

The Supreme Court's judgment in *Jeeja Ghosh* was a watershed moment for disability rights in India. It not only reinforced the

---

10. *Id.,* para 40
11. *Id.*, para 41
12. *Id.*, Para 46
13. *Id.*, paras 26–27

rights of disabled passengers in the aviation sector but also set a precedent for other public and private sectors to follow. The emphasis on training, infrastructure, and proper implementation of policies served as a blueprint for creating an inclusive environment for disabled persons. As the country moves forward, it is imperative that these legal protections translate into real-world changes, ensuring a more inclusive and equitable society for all.

The Battle Continues

The Supreme Court's judgment was a call to action for all stakeholders – the government, airlines, airport authorities, and society at large. It continues to be a reminder that while laws exist, their effective implementation requires a change in mindset and a commitment to inclusivity. But as we celebrate this victory, the reality is that even today, flying continues to remain a daunting, if not downright harrowing, experience for the disabled.

In May 2023, the staff of IndiGo Airlines refused to onboard an adolescent because he did not appear 'normal'.[14] This led the Directorate General of Civil Aviation (DGCA) slapping the carrier with a fine of ₹5 lakh and amend Section 3, Series M, Part I of the CAR, which now states:

> Airline shall not refuse carriage of any person on the basis of disability. However, in case an airline perceives that the health of such a passenger may deteriorate in-flight, the said passenger will have to be examined by a doctor, who shall categorically state the medical condition and whether the passenger is fit

14. Neha Tripathi, 'Airlines can no longer deny boarding to any person with disability' (*The Hindustan Times*, 4 June 2022), available at: https://www.hindustantimes.com/india-news/dgca-issues-norms-on-boarding-of-persons-with-disabilities-101654268544229.html (accessed 7 July 2024)

to fly or not. After obtaining the medical opinion, the airline shall take the appropriate call.[15]

The disabled have had to battle for their rights in the first world nations such as the United States as well, where Congress passed the Air Carrier Access Act (ACAA), prohibiting airlines from discriminating against passengers with disabilities on domestic and international flights, in 1986. The most recent survey from Paralyzed Veterans of America, a nonprofit organisation serving military veterans with spinal cord injuries and conditions, shows that one-fourth of Respondents said they had been injured transferring from their wheelchair to a narrower 'aisle chair'. In 2021, a passenger, Engracia Figueroa, developed ulcers from an improperly configured wheelchair replacement and died while waiting for United Airlines to repair and return the original chair.[16] This was in a country where 18.6 million Americans aged five and older have travel-limiting disabilities, as per a US Bureau of Transportation Statistics survey (2024).[17] After 40 years, the US Department of Transportation has now proposed amendments to the Air Carrier Access Act to enhance safety standards for airlines

15. Directorate General of Civil Aviation, 'Civil Aviation Requirements – Section 3, Series M, Part I', available at: https://www.dgca.gov.in/digigov-portal/?dynamicPage=dynamicPdf/MXLCjNkrsXP4ZtGtNaDOAg%3D%3D&main-null (accessed 7 July 2024)

16. Emily Alpert Reyes, 'An airline broke an activist's wheelchair. Her death months later amplified calls for change' (*Los Angeles Times, 6* June 2022), available at: https://www.latimes.com/california/story/2022-01-06/la-activist-broken-wheelchair-airlines-death (accessed 7 July 2024)

17. Bureau of Transportation Statistics, 'Travel Patterns of American Adults with Disabilities' (United States Department of Transportation, 18 April 2024), available at: https://www.bts.gov/travel-patterns-with-disabilities (accessed 7 July 2024)

serving travellers with disabilities.[18] The new rules would impose penalties on airlines for mishandling passenger mobility devices and mandate annual enhanced training for airline staff and contractors assisting passengers with disabilities and handling wheelchairs. Additionally, passengers would be able to select their preferred vendor for wheelchair and scooter repairs or replacements. These are measures that must be emulated by airlines across the world.

Stephen Hawking, the late physicist with ALS (Amyotrophic Lateral Sclerosis), a progressive neurogenerative disease, who is much acclaimed for his groundbreaking work on black holes and cosmology, put it best when he said, 'We have the moral duty to remove the barriers to participation, and to invest sufficient funding and expertise to unlock the vast potential of People with Disabilities.'

18. Lebawit Lily Girma, 'Flying with Disabilities Is a Dangerous Nightmare. But Change Is in the Air' (*Bloomberg,* 3 July2024), available at: https://www.bloomberg.com/news/articles/2024-07-03/flying-with-disabilities-could-be-getting-easier-by-end-of-2024 (accessed 7 July 2024)

Manraj Grewal Sharma

Manraj Grewal Sharma is the Resident Editor of *The Indian Express*, Chandigarh. Author of a book on Punjab militancy called *Dreams after Darkness*, she has also worked as a consulting editor with development organisations such as United Nations Environment Programme and Asia Pacific Adaptation Forum. She has been a publishing consultant with the Asian Development Bank, Manila as well, and was the managing editor of *Gender, Technology and Development*, an international peer-reviewed journal published by the Asian Institute of Technology, Bangkok, for five years.

Disability and Cinema – Addressing Negative Stereotypes and Shifting Narratives

Nipun Malhotra v. Sony Pictures Films India Private Limited

Sanjeev Sharma & Kritika Sharma

> We recognize that disability is central to diversity, that the disability community comprises one of the largest minority groups in our country, and that people with disabilities face exclusion in front of and behind the camera. We understand that increasing auditions, no matter the size of the role, is a critical step towards achieving inclusion in the industry. We will continue to champion and encourage more auditions for actors and actresses with disabilities on television and film.
>
> —*Ruderman Family Foundation Pledge*[1]

1. Ruderman Family Foundation, 'Pledge', available at: https://rudermanfoundation.org/pledge/ (accessed 29 December 2024)

Sony Pictures signed this pledge, becoming the fourth major filmmaker to sign the Ruderman Family Foundation's pledge.[2] Movies have a significant global impact on challenging and reshaping stereotypical impressions of disabled characters. Historically, such characters were often portrayed as helpless, villainous, or objects of pity and, at times, used solely to inspire able-bodied individuals or to evoke sympathy. However, recognising the fact that disability stems not from medical conditions but through social and economic barriers to participation,[3] films like *The Theory of Everything* (2014), which is based on the life of Stephen Hawking, who, despite being diagnosed with motor neuron disease at the age of 21, defeats all odds and achieves unprecedented success in the field of physics, as well as *CODA* 'Child Of Deaf Adults' (2021), portray characters with disabilities as multidimensional, emphasising their personal struggles, achievements, and humanity beyond their disability.

Other movies such as *A Beautiful Mind* (2001), which is about John Nash, a brilliant mathematician who goes on to win a Nobel Prize for his revolutionary work on game theory after being diagnosed and treated for paranoid schizophrenia, and *My Left Foot* (1989) where Christy Brown, diagnosed with Cerebral Palsy at birth affecting most of his body, learns to paint and write with the only unaffected limb in his body, his left foot, share with the audience the lived experiences of individuals with disabilities, encouraging empathy rather than pity. By placing audiences in the

---

2. Ruderman Family Foundation, 'Sony Pictures Entertainment Reaffirms Commitment to Actors with Disabilities in Partnership with the Ruderman Family Foundation' (3 September 2021), available at: https://rudermanfoundation.org/press_releases/sony-pictures-entertainment-reaffirms-commitment-to-actors-with-disabilities-in-partnership-with-the-ruderman-family-foundation/ (accessed 29 December 2024)

3. See for example, Lisa Waddington and Mark Priestly, 'A human rights approach to disability assessment' *Journal of International and Comparative Social Policy* (2021) 37(1) 1–15, 2

shoes of the characters, such movies help people understand the systemic challenges and internal resilience of disabled individuals.

The wholesome purpose is to break down social stigma and promote acceptance through fuller and more accurate portrayals of disability within cinema, which in itself can be a powerful tool to effectuate and channelise change. Movies like *Wonder* (2017), which is about August, a boy who suffers from a facial deformity and enters a private school in the fifth grade, enduring bullying from his peers yet finds a way to overcome them with his friends and family, and *Temple Grandin* (2010), which is a movie on Temple Grandin, who was diagnosed with autism as a child and now shares her ability to 'think in pictures', which helps her solve problems that neurotypical brains might miss, work towards such portrayals, highlighting diversity and greater understanding. *Temple Grandin,* for instance makes the case that the world needs people on the autism spectrum: visual thinkers, pattern thinkers, and verbal thinkers, amongst others.

These movies are examples of how disabled persons are accepted, combating stigmas surrounding visible and invisible disabilities. These films attempt to educate viewers about the prejudice that disabled people face and emphasise the importance of inclusion. Movies play a pivotal role, considering their reach through mainstream viewership as well as Over-The-Top (OTT) platforms as a means to reach viewers. Seeing authentic, non-stereotypical portrayals empowers disabled people and fosters a sense of belonging.

Part of this is linked to representation within cinema. When movies like *Sound of Metal* (2019) cast actors from the deaf community, it provides authentic representation and validates their voices. While purely fictional, Riz Ahmed portrays a heavy metal drummer's life, which is turned upside down when he begins to lose his hearing and must confront a future filled with silence.

Films can challenge societal narratives that equate worth with physical or mental ability. By normalising disability as part of human diversity, movies advocate for inclusion and accessibility. For example, the popularity of *CODA* (2021), which prominently featured deaf actors and sign language, spurred conversations on accessibility in cinema and other industries. The movie is about Ruby, who is the only family member with hearing in a deaf family from Gloucester, Massachusetts. At 17, she works mornings before school to help her parents and brother keep their fishing business afloat. But in joining her high school's choir club, Ruby finds herself drawn to both her duet partner and her latent passion for singing. Troy Michael Kotsur, who played Frank Rossi in CODA, was nominated for a Golden Globe Award and became the first deaf man to win an Academy Award for acting, winning the BAFTA (British Academy Film and Television Arts) Award and SAG (Screen Actors Guild) Award for this role.

With the global reach of streaming platforms, these narratives transcend borders, influencing cultural attitudes worldwide. Diverse portrayals of disability help challenge entrenched stereotypes, even in societies where the stigma against disability is more pronounced. Despite progress, underrepresentation and tokenism remain issues of concern. Authentic storytelling by disabled filmmakers and writers is still rare. To continue breaking stereotypes, the film industry must prioritise inclusivity behind the camera as much as on-screen.

Moving to Indian cinema and the case of *Nipun Malhotra v. Sony Pictures Films India Private Limited and Others.*[4] Within this context, the issue of accurate, multidimensional, and diverse portrayals of disability in cinema and how this is or could be done remains critical. This case is particularly relevant as it draws attention to

4. 2024 SCC OnLine SC 1639

how disabilities are portrayed in cinema, how they possibly ought to be, and how the law might, in fact, be insufficient in addressing an adequate shift from an ability-based or medical model to view disabilities to one based on human rights. The latter is based on Persons with Disabilities being seen as rights holders instead of being categorised as disabled on the basis of a medical or individual diagnosis. The human rights-based approach towards disability was highlighted as a priority by the Committee on the Convention on the Rights of Persons with Disabilities in their response to the Initial Report submitted by India before the Committee, asking that this shift in approach be taken into consideration and reflected in the country's national legislation (and policy).[5]

The Facts

The case was brought before the Supreme Court through an appeal against a judgment of the Delhi High Court, which dismissed a petition that was filed under Article 226. The Appellant, who himself is a person with arthrogryposis, was aggrieved by the manner of the portrayal of Persons with Disabilities in the film *Aankh Micholi*. The film depicts two families arranging a matrimonial alliance whilst concealing disabilities that many members of both families are afflicted with. According to the Appellant, the film violated constitutionally protected Rights of Persons with Disabilities through negative or pejorative depiction of disabled characters and through such depiction (of stereotypes associated with such disabilities), violated the 1952 Cinematograph Act and the 2016 Rights of Persons with Disabilities Act. As per the Appellant, by according the film a 'U' certification, the Central Board of Film

5. See UN Committee on the Rights of Persons with Disabilities, 'Concluding observations on the Initial Report of India' CRPD/C/IND/CO/1 (29 October 2019), 2

Certification (CBFC) failed its statutory duty 'to certify films following applicable guidelines'.[6]

The Appellant had issued notice to Sony Pictures, raising objections to the trailer on various counts of what he claimed to be misrepresentation and use of derogatory terms for characters who were Persons with Disabilities. He contended the trailer suggested that Persons with Disabilities ought to conceal these and that it reinforced stereotypes through misguided portrayals and promoted inequality, thus increasing misconceptions, bias, and prejudice, presenting Persons with Disabilities as subjects of comic relief and ridicule while failing to evoke empathy and promotion of inclusive and accurate presentation of disability. On the other hand, Sony Pictures refuted these contentions and claimed that the *overall message* of the film was one of overcoming the challenge of disability and the struggles faced by Persons with Disabilities and their families, and the efforts to overcome them. Sony Pictures contended that the film sought to dislodge the idea that disability obstructs a fulfilling life, claimed protection under freedom of speech and expression in addition to asserting that the film does not pity or look down upon the characters with disabilities in it but depicts their agency and skills, which is neither derogatory nor stereotypical.

The High Court, while noticing the primary challenge to the film as being offensive to the sensibilities of Persons with Disabilities, concluded that this was not the case. Considering that, in the meantime, the film had been granted certification for unrestricted public exhibition by the CBFC, it concluded that the reliefs were non-maintainable. The High Court reinforced its dismissal by the fact that there exist guidelines issued by the Central Government under Section 5B(2) of the Cinematograph Act, 1952, which

6. Guidelines for Certification of Films for Public Exhibition, 1991

include specific provisions for Persons with Disabilities and provide a comprehensive framework for film certification. The appeal against this decision reached the Supreme Court.

Relief Sought

Broadly, the Appellant sought directions that an expert on disabilities be included within the Central Board of Film Certification and a similar inclusion of an expert be made under the Cinematograph Act, 1952. The Appellant also sought an award of punitive damages from Sony Pictures to a charitable institution along with a public apology.

Rights Invoked

The guaranteed rights under the Rights of Persons with Disabilities Act (RPwD Act) of 2016, along with those contained in the Cinematograph Act, 1952, the Cinematograph (Certification) Rules, 1983, and the Guidelines for Certification of Films for Public Exhibition, 1991, built on the fundamental rights under Articles 14, 19, and 21 were invoked by both parties.

The Decision: Shifting Paradigms and Missed Opportunities?

The Supreme Court examined the matter in the background of the legislative framework, including the impact of the provisions of the RPwD Act 2016 on the certification of films under the Cinematograph Act.

After referring to the process under which certification is granted, the allegation of whether egregious portrayal of characters with disabilities requires judicially mandated checks and framing of guidelines for the creators of content was examined. The court found that the Board is required to view the film as a whole and not base its decision on isolated bits and scenes in the film. Once certified, the film is presumed to have complied with the applicable regulations and ordinarily cannot be re-assessed, considering that an expert body has already considered all aspects. This is based on the principle of slow interference by the court.[7] The certification of the film was, in any case, not questioned.

While examining the case for Sony Pictures, a filmmaker's right to exhibit films fell squarely within the fundamental right to freedom of speech and expression under Article 19(1)(a), which is subject to reasonable restrictions under Article 19(2). It is the Cinematograph Act 1952 that imposes such restrictions within the rubric of the terms 'decency and morality' stated under Article 19(2). The provisions of the 1952 Act, which impose restraints on cinematic speech, would naturally be narrowly constructed because of the potential to impair the significant value of free speech, which is constitutionally protected. This was held by the Supreme Court in *K.A. Abbas v. Union of India,*[8] where the court found that the effect of a film is to be seen from the vantage of an ordinary person of common sense rather than that of a hypersensitive person. Among the principles that must be borne in mind while deciding the fitness of a film for public exhibition are its social impact and social change, rather than orthodox notions, and it must be judged by its **overall message** and not on the basis of isolated depictions of social evils.

A significant contribution of this judgment is the court's emphasis on how, in dealing with cinematic speech, its context was considered paramount, and the court's view on the harmful and debilitating effects of the depiction of stereotypes associated with disability. This can also be seen in the court's approach towards the

7. *Supra* note 4, para 72.1

8. (1970) 2 SCC 780

use of language and of humour vis-à-vis disability. The court noted that a stereotypical portrayal of Persons with Disabilities channels attention to the medical aspects of impairment rather than the social aspects that disable a person. Such stereotypical views act as self-fulfilling prophecies,[9] as per the court, and add to the already existing negative assumptions about their abilities and resultantly exacerbate systemic inequalities and inhibit their dignified participation in the public sphere for education or employment. The court termed stereotypes as being the 'antithesis to dignity and non-discrimination' and traced safeguards against stereotyping to Article 15.[10]

The RPwD Act 2016 aligned the Indian law with the UN Convention on the Rights of Persons with Disabilities. It embodied principles of dignity, individual autonomy, non-discrimination, and effective participation, bringing a fundamental shift from viewing disability through a charity lens to that of a human rights perspective. The core is to empower Persons with Disabilities, allowing them full and effective participation in society. The court made specific reference to Article 4.3 of the UN Convention on the Rights of Persons with Disabilities in the context of raising awareness requiring the state parties to implement a systemic awareness-raising programme through media campaigns to portray positive images of Persons with Disabilities and on a broader level shift the perception of Persons with Disabilities from objects of charity to rights holders. The recent rulings referred to emphasised the role of courts in attempting to prevent stigmatisation and discrimination against individuals with disabilities, recognising the profound impact on their sense of identity and dignity.

---

9. *Supra* note 4, para 30

10. *Id.*, paras 32, 33

While recognising Article 19(1)(a) as 'perhaps the most precious of all freedoms guaranteed by our Constitution'[11] any expression which may confirm and strengthen people's prejudices against a group in question, which only marginalises and disenfranchises them, may not enjoy complete protection under this freedom. Deviating from the historically oppressive representation of persons where disability is mocked or joked about, such an understanding was found to be obsolete under the present social model that views disability as a function of social barriers that disable such individuals. The court made a distinction between what was termed as 'disability humour' (that which was empowered through a reclamation of public discourse) and 'disabling humour' (that which disables further through its negative connotation).

While balancing opposing views between the freedom of speech and expression with the fundamental rights under Articles 14, 15, and 21 of the Appellant, the Supreme Court noticed that the High Court chose not to engage in the discussion as to which right – that of freedom of speech (cinematic speech) or the Rights of Persons with Disabilities – would take precedence. This was primarily because the Appellant had not contested the claim of Sony Pictures that the **overall message** of the film was about the resilience of persons with disability and that the primary challenge that the film offended sensibilities was not established. Keeping in line with the observation made earlier in the case of *Indibly*,[12] the Supreme Court concluded that the freedom under Article 19(1)(a) does not include the freedom to lampoon, stereotype, misrepresent, or disparage those already marginalised. If the **overall message** of the work infringes the Rights of Persons with Disabilities, it is not protected speech, obviating the need for any balancing. However,

11. *Id.*, para 62

12. *Indibily Creative (P) Ltd. v. State of W.B.*, (2020) 12 SCC 436

in appropriate cases, if a stereotypical/disparaging portrayal is justified for the overall message of the film, the right to retain such a portrayal will have to be balanced against the fundamental and statutory rights of those portrayed.

In conclusion, it could not be universally accepted in all circumstances that freedom of speech and expression would take precedence. It would have to be balanced with the nature of the portrayal in the overall aim of the movie. At the same time, the court issued specific recommendations that act as a framework for the accurate portrayal of disability within cinema. A recommendation was made that Persons with Disabilities be consulted in the creation of such projects in various ways, such as through the inclusion of experts.[13] The court left it to the Board, which has experts, to decide on the issue of whether films depicting disability met such standards or warranted a balancing of the two rights of free cinematic speech and the rights to equality, non-discrimination, and dignity. The framework issued by the court was in line with the judgment in *Vikash Kumar.* The framework highlighted the significance of language in this regard, such as how certain words that cultivate institutional discrimination and language that individualise impairment and overlook disabling social barriers should be avoided. It called for creators to check for an accurate representation of medical conditions to avoid misleading portrayals of impairments. The court called for a balanced representation of persons with disability that showcases not only their challenges but also successes in a multidimensional and authentic way in order to share with the audiences their lived experiences. Finally, the court highlighted the value of participation and that decision-making bodies would be advised to bear in mind the values of participation while also simultaneously implementing training and sensitisation

13. *Supra* note 4, para 72.5

programs on the topic of disability for individuals involved in creating visual art content. However, it did not direct the State to address areas of non-implementation, nor did it ask during the proceedings, for information on such implementing guidelines and procedures, pointing out how further measures might be needed to implement a shift in approaches towards disability – towards a human rights approach – such as acknowledging the need for non-physical factors in creating an enabling environment or a 'barrier-free environment', and the gap in implementation, which has also been pointed out by the Committee on the UN Convention on the Rights of Persons with Disabilities.[14]

A Human Rights-Based Approach towards Disability

The judgment makes inroads where *Vikash Kumar v. Union Public Service Commission and Others*[15] left off. *Vikash Kumar* was restricted to the right to employment in the context of benchmark disabilities; the court, while recognising disability in the context of the provisions of the Rights of Persons with Disabilities Act, 2016 (RPwD), held that the Act laid a foundation for a more expansive affirmative duty which went beyond mere non-discrimination going on to an obligation on the Government to taking appropriate steps to utilise the capacity of Persons with Disabilities. The use of the words 'suffering' and 'disease', while referring to disability, was unwarranted, and viewing disability as an affliction causing suffering or God-given is rooted in medical models of disability, and such insensitive language offends human dignity or persons with such disability. The present judgment emphasises a necessary shift from the medical model of disability to one that takes into consideration social and economic factors that act as barriers

14. *Supra* note 5

15. (2021) 5 SCC 370

to participation for Persons with Disabilities and views them as rights holders – a human rights-based approach. Such an approach highlights the diversity in disability and disabling factors and is more suitable as a lens to view disability than the medical model, which focuses on impairment and creates a narrative of Persons with Disabilities being objects of pity and care.

The judgment extensively examines the entire spectrum of how disability is treated under the charter of laws both in India and universally, including various UN conventions, but in conclusion, what gets highlighted is the inability of the law to bring about social change. The inadequate societal impact of laws reflects the inability to bring about the needed change through judicial intervention. Thus, the answer possibly falls outside of the law, to a shift in narratives and paradigms, to consistently and effectively shift to a human rights-based approach towards disability.

The Power of Cinema to Establish Narratives: Portraying the Multitudes of Disability

Cinema can act as a conduit for social change. Movies have the power to affect change in the attitudes of viewers, including their perception of disabilities, improving such perceptions in areas concerning employability, etc.[16] A study conducted on the attitudes of individuals without disabilities before and after watching a movie about a police officer with paraplegia highlighted that the movie increased the viewers' awareness concerning disability and the eligibility of Persons with Disabilities for various forms

16. Jan D. Reinhardt, Andrew Pennycott, and Bernd A.G. Fellinghauer, 'Impact of a film portrayal of a police officer with spinal cord injury on attitudes towards disability: a media effects experiment' (2014) 36(4) *Disability and Rehabilitation* 289–294

of employment, including within the police forces.[17] Careful representation of Persons with Disabilities within varied visual media, including graphic novels or *manga*, for example, has been linked to greater awareness of disability.[18]

By portraying the multidimensional lives of persons who are disabled, cinema and visual media, more generally, could help shift public discourse around disability from pity or inability to one of empowerment. It can help raise important questions such as: Is disability to be ridiculed? Something that must remain a secret? To be ashamed of? Do such thoughts stem from a feeling of disappointment? Of shame? Inability to fit in? Can it also be said that this description comes from those who consider themselves as able-bodied and thus constitute the vast majority who consider themselves normal? Can it be said that one tends to deprecate anyone who does not fit into a tight compartment of what is perceived as normal? Approximately 1.3 billion qualify as being disabled in one form or another. How does this affect society from both sides? These are some of the questions that come to mind.

Conclusion

Movies are powerful tools for changing perceptions, and the Supreme Court highlights this by analysing the powerful impact – both negative and positive – that movies can have on public discourse on disability. They can empower and uplift when they include actors and participants from members of the community, depicting the lived experiences of persons who are disabled and showcasing authentic portrayals of Persons with Disabilities leading

17. *Ibid.*

18. On how 'carefully selected manga can teach us about disability from an unconventional perspective', see for example, Yoshiko Okuyama, *Reframing Disability in Manga* (University of Hawaii Press, 2020)

full and multidimensional lives. They can also exacerbate the challenges faced by Persons with Disabilities, where such movies perpetuate stereotypes for the sake of such negative portrayals, further debilitating the experiences of such individuals within society. Thus, the guidelines of the court vis-à-vis accurate and careful portrayals of disability in visual media are a significant step. However, to ensure that these are meaningful in ameliorating the portrayal of disability in visual media and effecting contribution to greater awareness, these must be coupled with proactive measures both within the cinematic community itself as well as through further implementation measures by the State in ensuring that these facilitate a shift to a human rights-based approach towards disability. While there is still a long way to go, films that authentically portray persons with disability as multifaceted individuals contribute to a more inclusive and empathetic world.

◇◇

Major Sanjeev Sharma & Kritika Sharma

On completing his schooling from The Lawrence School, Sanawar, **Sanjeev Sharma** completed his LLB from Panjab University – joined the Bar at Himachal Pradesh High Court, and then went on to serve with the Judge Advocate General's Department of the Indian Army, discharging the role of a Trial Judge and advising field commanders on matters of military law. After seeking premature release in the rank of Major, he took up his private practice, transferring to Chandigarh in 1996. In 2009, he was designated by the High Court as a Senior Advocate. He has held various positions, including that of Additional Advocate General for the State of Punjab. The Governor of Punjab and Administrator of Union Territory, Chandigarh, appointed him as the Senior Standing Counsel for the Union Territory of Chandigarh as well as the Senior Standing Counsel for the Chandigarh Housing Board. Later, the High Court appointed him as a Senior Counsel for its litigation. With over 40 years of experience, he has represented the States of Punjab, Haryana, the Union Territory of Chandigarh, and the State of Himachal Pradesh in critical litigation. He is also currently running his ninth year as the Editor of the Indian Law Reporter – Punjab Haryana High Court. His experience is rich in the field of Constitutional law as well as Arbitration, including International Commercial Arbitration, and taking on advisory roles for several corporations. He serves on the Advisory Board of Manav Rachna University (Law), Faridabad. He has been on the Board of Governors of the Lawrence School, Sanawar, and Chairman of its Estate and Legal Committee. He was the first Chairman of the Advocates Welfare Fund Committee and remained the Secretary of the Senior Advocates' Association twice at the Punjab and Haryana High Court.

Kritika Sharma has completed her PhD at Leiden University, the Netherlands. Her doctoral thesis was on the governance of the International Criminal Court (ICC) by the Assembly of States Parties (ASP) to the Rome Statute at Leiden University. She holds an LLB with Honors from Amity Law School (India) and an Advanced LLM in Public International Law with a specialisation in International Criminal Law from Leiden University (*cum laude*). She was awarded the International Court of Justice (ICJ) Judicial Fellowship in 2017 by Leiden University and subsequently worked at the ICJ as a Judicial Fellow for the year 2017–2018. She was a Research Fellow in the Department of International Law and Dispute Resolution at the Max Planck Institute Luxembourg for International, European, and Regulatory Procedural Law between 2019 and 2024, as well as a researcher at the Luxembourg Centre for European Law (LCEL) between January and October 2024. She was a Research Assistant for the Independent Expert Review of the ICC in 2020 and has previously interned at the ICC, the

ICJ, and the Coalition for the ICC. Her research focuses on international criminal law, international institutional law, and legal theory, and she has authored various peer-reviewed publications within this field. Kritika has been a Convenor of the Minerva LAW Network, an initiative that is part of the Max Planck Law Network, since 2020 and has worked in various editorial roles, including as Assistant Editor for the *Leiden Journal of International Law* (2016–2017), Copy and Language Editor for the *Groningen Journal of International Law* (2018–2019), and as an Associate Editor for the *Max Planck Encyclopedia for International Procedural Law* (2019–2024).

The Suffering Beneath the Tough Façade – Disabilities in the Military

Ashish Kumar Chauhan v. Commanding Officer

Arjun Sheoran & Major D.P. Singh

The Background

In the grand tapestry of national narratives, stories of valour and sacrifice often steal the spotlight, leaving the quieter, more painful battles in the shadows. The annals of Indian military history are rife with examples of our brave soldiers, who, while hailed for their bravery on the battlefield, are often left rudderless in the treacherous ocean of the Indian legal system, fighting for justice against an indifferent system for their basic rights. The tragedy is further compounded when it involves soldiers who have been rendered disabled during service, whether with external injuries directly in the line of duty or with invisible disabilities, the suffering of which is not fathomable to the public at large and which is not holistically recognised by the system itself, including their own colleagues in uniform.

The subject of disability pension and other monetary benefits to soldiers is paradoxically one where, although on the surface, all stakeholders seem to be in favour of granting such benefits, but once we lift the curtain, what is revealed is a murky world of systemic apathy and cryptic policy infrastructure.

The disability and death payouts in the defence services are governed by the Entitlement Rules,[1] as amended from time to time. Under these rules, the scope of diseases/disabilities covered is substantially wide. The rules define the nature of injuries and/or diseases that entitle the claimant to disability benefits. An important limb of these provisions is Rule 9 of the 1982 Rules, which provides that the benefit of the doubt would lie in favour of the claimant. It has been a common refrain, as reflected in judicial dicta, that while the rules are quite liberal, these are interpreted restrictively by those in the establishment. However, the major issue that remains a bone of contention is, that as per the interpretation of the system, for any claim to succeed, any disablement/death has to be certified by the appropriate medical authority as being 'attributable to or aggravated by military service.' The fulcrum of the quagmire, however, as pointed out in the Ministry of Defence's Committee of Experts Report published in 2015[2] under the aegis of the Raksha Mantri, of which one of us (Major D.P. Singh) was a member, titled *Review of Service and Pension Matters Including Potential Disputes, Minimizing Litigation and Strengthening Institutional Mechanisms Related to Redressal of Grievances*, is reflected in the following passage:

> The problem however, is that the rigid interpretation and application of said rules in a literal, unscientific, and

---

1. Entitlement Rules for Casualty Pensionary Awards, 1982, available at: https://desw.gov.in/sites/default/files/ER-1982.pdf

2. Ministry of Defence Report, 2015, available at: https://www.mod.gov.in/dod/sites/default/files/Reportc051020_0.pdf

> mathematical manner and issuance of contradictory local instructions are leading to denial of disability benefits by incorrectly declaring disabilities 'Neither Attributable Nor Aggravated by military service' (NANA) which are otherwise authorised to be eligible for benefits under the rules. Apart from leading to denial of disability benefits, this also results in denial of any form of pension and consequently, a dignified life if the disability of a person discharged with less than pensionable service is declared NANA.

The committee went on to discuss various facets of the issue and further observed:

> While dealing with the disabilities of military personnel, the much-argued comparison with an ordinary person is not based on a sound footing. There are times when it is remarked that such a disease may also have arisen had the particular person not been in the Army. The Committee notes that there can be no comparison of the inherent stress and strain of military life with a civilian employee or others, and what may be 'lifestyle diseases' for a common person on the street may be aggravated by stress and strain in the case of military personnel. A person who is 24 hours/365 days on call, sometimes under the shadow of a gun, under a strict disciplinary code, mostly away from his family, in a strictly regimented routine, cannot be simplistically compared with a civilian employee. The nature of military service denies to all military personnel a commune living with his family or in his hometown, the enjoyment of gazetted holidays and even the enjoyment of normal day-to-day freedoms such as the very basic liberties of life which are taken by all citizens for granted… It is surprising that once even the apex medical

body, that is, the Medical Services Advisory Committee (MSAC) has itself conceded that, medically speaking, almost all such disabilities are affected by military service, which is also a universally accepted military norm, then why should other authorities be allowed to override the said reality. When it is also accepted by all stakeholders that the life expectancy of members of the military is much lower than civilian employees, then there should remain no controversy on the effect of military service on the health of individuals. In any case, such instances are contemptuous to the decisions of the Supreme Court, and we must remind here that under Article 144 of the Constitution, all authorities are to bow down to the majesty of the law laid down by the Supreme Court and act in the aid of the Supreme Court. The health of our troops, our responsibility towards our veterans, and the lesser life expectancy of our soldiers and veterans cannot be measured in monetary terms or by denying them minor amounts that they are fully entitled to under the rules. Even as back as in 1982, the Constitution Bench of the Supreme Court in D.S. Nakara's case had endorsed the securing of socio-economic justice in a rapidly growing and flourishing State which can afford such benefits which are anyway admissible under law.

As the report, and indeed many judgments of the Supreme Court and High Courts, as also the Armed Forces Tribunal, have noted, the inherent stress and strain of military service lead to the aggravation of disabilities in defence personnel. Characteristics of service such as constant movement, living away from family, curtailment of freedoms, posting in hostile environments, and the like, affect the health profile of soldiers, but most of the disabilities incurred by them are branded 'Neither Attributable Nor Aggravated by military service' thereby leading to heartburn and also unnecessary litigation, with the Ministry of Defence trying its best to wear out the litigants till the highest court of the land. Some disabilities, like injuries suffered in the line of duty, are visible; some, such as heart diseases, mental health issues, spinal afflictions, hearing loss, etc., are unseen and away from the public gaze.

The Case

We seek to analyse the judgment of the Supreme Court in *Ashish Kumar Chauhan v. Commanding Officer*[3] to assess the indignity accorded to our soldiers by systemic lapses. Though the tale of Ashish Kumar Chauhan, a former Corporal in the Indian Air Force, whose life was irrevocably altered not by the battlefield but by a blood transfusion that came laced with an unseen enemy—HIV (human immunodeficiency viruses), is somewhat different than the usual cases of disability benefits that the courts have now been flooded with by the Ministry of Defence and the Defence Services, yet there is a common thread of litigation till the Supreme Court which places it in the same box. His journey through the labyrinth of military healthcare and the Indian legal system is not just a fight for justice but a poignant reminder of the invisible wars fought by many soldiers.

During Operation Parakram, Chauhan, a radar operator stationed at the 302 Transportable Radar Unit in Pathankot, was diagnosed with severe symptomatic anaemia and was admitted to the 171 Military Hospital in Samba. The hospital, set up as an ad-hoc facility during the operation, lacked a fully equipped blood bank. Under the circumstances, a unit of blood was transfused into Chauhan's veins, a routine procedure that, unbeknownst to him, marked the beginning of a long and painful struggle. It wasn't

3. (2023) 15 SCC 152

until 2014, twelve years after the transfusion, that Chauhan was diagnosed with HIV. Chauhan's efforts to trace the origin of his infection led him to believe that the 2002 blood transfusion was the likely source. However, accessing records and seeking accountability within the labyrinthine structure of military administration proved to be an uphill battle.

Chauhan's quest for justice led him to file a complaint with the National Consumer Disputes Redressal Commission (NCDRC), seeking compensation for what he alleged was medical negligence. The demand was a staggering ₹95.03 crore, a figure that underscored the severity of the personal and professional damage he had suffered. However, the NCDRC dismissed his complaint, citing a lack of expert testimony to substantiate his claims. Refusing to accept defeat, Chauhan escalated the matter to the Supreme Court of India. The Supreme Court's deliberations brought critical issues to the forefront, including the responsibilities of military medical facilities and the implementation of the HIV and AIDS (Prevention and Control) Act, 2017.

The Supreme Court's judgment in *Ashish Kumar Chauhan* was a landmark moment, with the court recognising the lapses in the medical treatment Chauhan received, particularly the inadequacies in the ad-hoc blood bank's procedures at the 171 Military Hospital. The Court of Inquiry had found that while the blood was screened as per the standards of the time, there was a significant failure in documenting and investigating the incident properly.

The judgment underscored the immense mental and emotional distress Chauhan endured. The systemic failures and bureaucratic hurdles only exacerbated his suffering, highlighting the need for a more empathetic approach to handling such cases. The ₹1.54 crore compensation finally awarded by the Supreme Court was not merely financial relief but also a symbolic recognition of the injustices he faced.

The case also spotlighted the HIV and AIDS (Prevention and Control) Act, 2017, a critical piece of legislation aimed at protecting the rights of people living with HIV. The Act's provisions on informed consent, confidentiality, and non-discrimination were central to the court's considerations, emphasising the importance of their robust implementation within all institutions, including the military.

Chauhan's case also sheds light on broader issues that extend beyond the individual to the systemic and institutional levels. It raises critical questions about the adequacy of healthcare and support systems for military personnel, the implementation of legal protections for people living with HIV, and the societal attitudes towards chronic illness and disability.

However, most importantly, the Supreme Court made a telling observation regarding the peculiar and far-reaching impact of a hyper-technical and apathetic approach while dealing with disabilities in the Armed Forces, going as far as to say:

> People sign up to join the Armed Forces with considerable enthusiasm and a sense of patriotic duty. This entails a conscious decision to put their lives on the line and be prepared for the ultimate sacrifice of their lives. A corresponding duty is cast upon all state functionaries, including echelons of power within the Armed Forces, to ensure that the highest standards of safety (physical/mental wellbeing, medical fitness, as well as wellness) are maintained. This is absolutely the minimum required of the military/air force employer for not only assuring the morale of the forces but also showing the sense of how such personnel matter and their lives count, which reinforces their commitment and confidence. Any flagging from these standards – as the multiple instances in the present case have established, only entails a loss of confidence in the personnel, undermines their morale, and injects a sense

> of bitterness and despair not only to the individual concerned but to the entire force, leaving a sense of injustice. When a young person from either sex (as is nowadays the case) enrols or joins any Armed Forces, at all times, their expectation is to be treated with dignity and honour. The present case has demonstrated again and again how dignity, honour, and compassion towards the appellant were completely lacking in behaviour by the respondent employer. Repeatedly, the record displays a sense of disdain and discrimination, even a hint of stigma attached to the appellant, in the attitude of the respondent employer. Although this court has attempted to give tangible relief, at the end of the day, it realises that no amount of compensation in monetary terms can undo the harm caused by such behaviour, which has shaken the foundation of the appellant's dignity, robbed him of honour, and rendered him not only desperate even cynical.[4]

This is only the latest in a series of judgments by the Supreme Court as well as different High Courts across the country, wherein the claims of soldiers suffering disability or disease as a result of, or in the course of service have been allowed while denigrating the hyper-technical and flawed approach of the Medical Boards. This shows that our soldiers, despite serving and suffering in such service of the nation, often get relief only after knocking on the doors of the courts, a process that can often take years and cause untold suffering.

Supreme Court's Jurisprudence

The Supreme Court, in *Dharamvir Singh v. Union of India and Others,*[5] allowed the claim for disability pension of a sepoy,

---

4. *Id.,* para 103

5. 2013 (7) SCC 316

released from service with 20% permanent disability as he was found suffering from Generalised Seizures (Epilepsy), which had been rejected by the Medical Board on the ground that the said disability could neither be considered attributable nor aggravated by military service. The court discussed in great detail the different provisions of the Rules. The court held that in case a person incurs a disability while in service, it is deemed to be service-related unless it is recorded that it was existing at the time of entry into service or the medical board states that it was a condition that could not be detected at the time of entry into service. The court also emphasised that the benefit of the doubt operates in favour of disabled soldiers, and the onus of proof does not lie on the soldiers to prove their claims.

Disorders like those in the above case incurred in service, as well as others linked with mental health, form a substantial percentage of disabilities leading to boarding out of soldiers or disabled personnel serving with such disabilities till their discharge or superannuation and then living with such disabilities for the rest of their lives. However, at the same time, these cases are foremost in instances of rejection of claims for disability pension and other entitlements, with the Medical Board in most cases opining that the said disability is neither attributable to nor aggravated by military service and is rather constitutional, congenital, idiopathic, or unrelated to service. This is clearly adding insult to injury, as not only does the soldier face social stigma, but also has to run from pillar to post for his entitlements. In *Veerpal Singh v. Secretary, Ministry of Defence,*[6] a three-judge bench of the Supreme Court undertook a detailed discussion on the meaning and contours of schizophrenia among military personnel and directed a medical re-assessment of the soldier to be undertaken when he questioned

6. 2013 (8) SCC 83

his diagnosis. The bench discarded the approach professed by the government that the medical board consists of experts whose views cannot be questioned. The bench opined that such views might be worthy of respect but not worship.

The view of non-attributability of mental health issues mostly professed by the military medical boards was also soundly rejected by the Supreme Court in the case of *K. Srinivasa Reddy v. Union of India*,[7] in which it has been underlined that there was an aggravating factor of the disability of the solider since he was torn between the call of duty on one side and the illness of his father and domestic commitments on the other. The court observed that:

> A careful reading of the above would show that even if the disease was triggered in the circumstance set out by the respondents in the passage extracted above, it could not be said to be wholly unconnected to military service. The Medical Board in our opinion failed to keep the circumstances which appear to have triggered the disease in mind while holding that the disease was not attributable nor aggravated by the military service. The circumstances sufficiently suggest that the illness of the appellant's father and his commitment to the family on the one hand and the call of duty on the other played a major role in his contracting the disease that eventually led to his release from Army.

A guiding principle for Medical Boards was rightly provided by the Supreme Court while deciding a bunch of appeals in the case of *Union of India v. Rajbir Singh*,[8] where it was held:

---

7. Civil Appeal No. 5140 of 2011 decided on 09 October 2014, available at: https://indiankanoon.org/doc/127136638/ (accessed 15 September 2024)

8. (2015) 12 SCC 264

> Last but not the least is the fact that the provision for payment of disability pension is a beneficial provision which ought to be interpreted liberally so as to benefit those who have been sent home with a disability at times even before they completed their tenure in the Armed Forces. There may indeed be cases, where the disease was wholly unrelated to military service, but, in order that denial of disability pension can be justified on that ground, it must be affirmatively proved that the disease had nothing to do with such service. The burden to establish such a disconnect would lie heavily upon the employer for otherwise the rules raise a presumption that the deterioration in the health of the member of the service is on account of military service or aggravated by it. **A soldier cannot be asked to prove that the disease was contracted by him on account of military service or was aggravated by the same. The very fact that he was upon proper physical and other tests found fit to serve in the army should rise as indeed the rules do provide for a presumption that he was disease-free at the time of his entry into service.**[9] (emphasis added)

The judgments discussed above, particularly the observations made by the Supreme Court in *Ashish Kumar Chauhan,* become all the more relevant in the face of the Government's decision to amend the 1982 Rules in 2008, which was controversially undertaken by not following the process as per the Rules of Business, and then again recently in 2023, which led to widespread criticism in the echelons of retired and serving members of the Armed Forces. The new guidelines are called the *Entitlement Rules of Casualty Pension and Disability Compensation Award to Armed Forces Personnel, 2023.* The new rules have revised the

9. *Id.*, para 15

types of disabilities, replaced the term 'disability element' with 'impairment relief', and replaced the existing norms on disability pensions for Armed Forces personnel. In addition, the definition, calculation method, and eligibility criteria have also changed. This has led to fears, which are well-founded, that rather than curing the lacunae in the already existing policy, the new rules would effectively further narrow the scope of disability or death benefits since most medical conditions will not be regarded as 'attributable to, or aggravated by military service', which is a prerequisite for the said benefits. Interestingly, the new rules have brought down the percentage of disabilities in most diseases, some quite drastically, from, for example, 30% to 5%, as if a different kind of medical science applies to military personnel or if medical science or the nature of stress and strain of military service and the harsh practicalities of military life can be changed by simply amending the rules. The new guidelines have also introduced improbable and mathematical applications that are impossible to meet. For example, in order to be eligible for disability or death benefits for a heart attack, the solider should have served in severely stressful situations for a continuous period of more than 90 days in a high-altitude area, while there was no such condition in the past and there is no such condition even today for members of the Central Armed Police Forces. Rather, the rules till now provided that serving in a peace or field area had no connection with the attributability of a disability or death to military service.

Concluding Remarks

The above discussion clearly shows that in the case of military disabilities, as is often the case with the disbursement of benefits and entitlements under various welfare legislations in the country, the process often becomes a punishment. What is then required is a more efficient and streamlined ecosystem to ensure that the soldiers who put their lives and well-being at risk for the country are, in return, treated with the dignity and honour that their sacrifices behove. In an ideal world, the authorities would have been more concerned about the health of our soldiers and improving the same than fighting their disability and death benefits in judicial bodies all across India. The very thought of this is repulsive, but then this is the reality. Away from those stories of valour and sacrifice, our troops continue to defend a battle waged by their own, not on the borders, but in courtrooms spread all over the country.

Arjun Sheoran & Major D.P. Singh

Arjun Sheoran is an Advocate practicing before the Punjab and Haryana High Court. He is the Managing Partner of a boutique law firm, *Vaakya Legal*, which has offices in Chandigarh, Mumbai, and Toronto (Canada). He is an alumnus of the National Law School, Bangalore. He was the Deputy Advocate General for the State of Punjab from 2022 to 2024. He has remained associated with many social causes and issues of public interest during his professional career.

Major D.P. Singh (Devender Pal Singh) is a 100% war-disabled officer who was invalided out of the Army in 2007. He was left for dead during Operation Vijay (Kargil) but miraculously survived and created many landmarks in what he calls his 'second life'. He is also a motivational speaker and the first Indian amputee to run a marathon. He is known as the 'Indian Blade Runner'. In 2011, Major D.P. Singh initiated an NGO, 'The Challenging Ones'

(TCO), for Indian amputees, which now has 3,000 members. Many of such amputees are participating in sports and achieving personal excellence. He has been recognised and honoured internationally and was also a part of the Committee of Experts in 2015, constituted by the Late Mr Manohar Parrikar, India's then Defence Minister, to reduce litigation initiated by the Ministry of Defence against its serving and retired personnel. He is the recipient of five Limca Records and is also a National Awardee, wherein he was conferred with the National Award in the Role-Model category by the Ministry of Social Justice and Empowerment of the Government of India. In 2019, *Grit: The Major Story*, a biographical novel based on his life, was published by Hachette.

Do Persons with Disabilities Have the Right to Reservation in Promotion?

State of Kerala v. Leesamma Joseph

Raj Kumar Makkad & Himani Makkad

> I am only one; but still I am one. I cannot do everything, but still I can do something; I will not refuse to do something I can do.
>
> —*Edward Everett Hale, referring to his cousin Helen Keller*[1]

The above-stated quote by Edward Everett Hale, while referring to the disability rights advocate, the Late Helen Keller, resonates deeply with the struggles of Persons with Disabilities worldwide, particularly in India. Despite India being a signatory to the United Nations Convention on the Rights of Persons with Disabilities since 2007, significant challenges remain. Addressing a few of these challenges, the Supreme Court of India, in the case of *State of Kerala v. Leesamma Joseph*,[2] delivered a landmark judgment on the Rights of Persons with Disabilities (PwD) in relation to reservation in promotions in employment. This judgment was delivered on 28 June 2021 by a two-

1. Cited in *Jeeja Ghosh v. Union of India*, (2016) 7 SCC 761
2. (2021) 9 SCC 208

judge Bench comprising Justices Sanjay Kishan Kaul and Subhash Reddy. This commentary aims to dissect the judgment, discuss the application of reservation in promotion for Persons with Disabilities as per the Persons with Disabilities (Equal Opportunities, Protection of Rights and Full Participation) Act, 1995 (The 1995 Act), analyse its implications, and place it within the broader context of disability rights and affirmative action in India.

Factual Background

Leesamma Joseph, the Respondent, was appointed as a Typist/Clerk in the Police Department on compassionate grounds following the death of her brother. Suffering from Post-Polio Residual Paralysis (L) Lower Limb, her disability was assessed at 55%. She successfully cleared departmental tests for promotion and was promoted through various ranks. She was initially promoted to Lower Division Clerk in July 2001, Senior Clerk in September 2004, and later to Cashier in May 2015. However, she claimed that she was entitled to earlier promotions with consequential benefits based on the reservation provisions under the 1995 Act.

Background of Proceedings

The decision in *Leesamma Joseph* arose from a series of proceedings involving the Respondent's claim for reservation in promotions under the 1995 Act. The case sheds light on the Respondent's journey through the Kerala Administrative Tribunal and the Kerala High Court, which ultimately led to a legal debate in the Supreme Court regarding the rights of PwD in matters of promotion.

Kerala Administrative Tribunal

The matter was earlier filed by Leesamma Joseph before the Kerala Administrative Tribunal, which dismissed her application by order dated 27 February 2015.[3] The Tribunal's key observations were that the 1995 Act, specifically Sections 32 and 33, did not explicitly provide for reservations in promotions for PwD. These provisions only mandated identification and reservation of posts for direct recruitment. The Tribunal analysed the Bombay High Court's decision in National Confederation for Development of Disabled v. Union of India,4 which had directed reservation in promotions and held that Kerala Government's orders and general recruitment rules did not extend the reservation to promotional posts. The Tribunal ultimately observed that the Respondent's claim for reservation in promotions was not supported by the existing legal framework and dismissed her application accordingly.

Kerala High Court

The High Court, while allowing the appeal and setting aside the order of the Kerala Administrative Tribunal vide order dated 9 March 2020[5] held that reservation for the persons having physical disability would be applicable for promotions too, by relying upon the decisions of *Rajeev Kumar Gupta v. Union of India*[6] and *Siddaraju v. State of Karnataka*[7] wherein the courts affirmed that such reservation is applicable to promotions. The court granted notional benefits to Leesamma from the entitled date.

Aggrieved by the aforesaid judgment of the Kerala High Court, the State of Kerala approached the Supreme Court by filing an appeal. By the time the judgment came for arguments before the

---

3. O.A. NO.343/2015 titled *Leesamma Joseph v. State of Kerala and Others*

4. 2015 SCC OnLine Bom 5112

5. OP(KAT) No.286 OF 2015(Z)

6. (2016) 13 SCC 153

7. (2020) 19 SCC 572

Supreme Court, Leesamma Joseph had superannuated from her service; therefore, the Supreme Court was pleased to uphold the judgment passed by the High Court of Kerala so far as the right to reservation and monetary benefits are concerned, however, keeping in view the importance of various connected factors, a detailed judgment was passed based upon the following issues:

> Whether the 1995 Act requires reservations in promotions for Persons with Disabilities?
>
> Whether the implementation of reservation under Section 33 of the 1995 Act is contingent upon the identification of posts as outlined in Section 32?
>
> Whether a person with a disability can be denied promotion in the absence of a specific provision in the Rules for reservation in promotion?
>
> Whether the Respondent is eligible for promotion under the benefit of reservation as a person with a disability, even though she was not initially appointed under the PwD quota?

The Issues

Mandate of Reservations in Promotions for PwD under the 1995 Act

The Supreme Court's analysis of this issue hinges on the interpretation of Sections 32, 33, and 47 of the 1995 Act. The court emphasised upon Section 47 as this Section prohibits the reduction in rank or termination of an employee who acquires a disability during service. Specifically, it mandates that such employees, if unfit for their current role, must be shifted to another post with the same pay scale and benefits. Furthermore, no promotion shall be denied on the grounds of disability, ensuring equal opportunities for career progression. The court held that Sections 32 and 33 need to be read in conjunction with Section 47 to fully realise the legislative intent of non-discrimination and equal opportunity in government employment. This reading supports the conclusion that reservation in promotion is indeed mandated, aligning with the broader goals of the 1995 Act. The court further emphasised that the legislative mandate is clear: denying promotions to PwD would undermine the very purpose of the Act. Such denial would lead to stagnation and frustration among PwD, contrary to the Act's aim of fostering career progression and inclusivity. It was emphasised by the Supreme Court while dealing with this issue that Section 33 of the 1995 Act mandates that every establishment shall provide not less than 3% reservation in recruitment. The word recruitment cannot be narrowed down just to direct recruitment, as held by *Rajeev Kumar Gupta.*

The Supreme Court's judgment unequivocally clarified that the 1995 Act mandates reservations in promotions for PwD, provided the necessary conditions are met. The court discussed that reservations must be applied to the total number of vacancies in the cadre strength without distinguishing between direct recruitment and promotion. This holistic approach ensures that PwD receive equitable treatment across all levels of employment. The court laid down that two key conditions must be met for reservations in promotions:

Existence of Rules for Promotion: The rules must provide for promotion from the feeder cadre to the promotional posts.

Identification of Posts: Posts within the promotional cadre must be identified as suitable for PwD, as stipulated under Section 32 of the 1995 Act.

The Supreme Court's decision aligns with earlier judgments, such as those in *Government of India v. Ravi Prakash Gupta*[8] and *Union of India v. National Federation of the Blind.*[9] These cases reiterated that reservations should be computed based on the total number of vacancies, encompassing both direct recruitment and promotions. Additionally, the Bombay High Court's decision in *National Confederation for Development of Disabled v. Union of India*[10] supported this interpretation, which was endorsed by the Supreme Court, as emphasised above.

Dependency of Section 33 Reservations on Identification of Posts under Section 32

The Supreme Court's analysis of this issue, prompted by a plea from the *Amicus Curiae*, underscores a crucial point: the legislative intent behind the 1995 Act, which was never to allow Section 32 to be used as a barrier to the benefits of reservation provided under Section 33. The Supreme Court acknowledged that the identification of posts, as mandated by Section 32, is a prerequisite for implementing reservations under Section 33. However, this prerequisite should not be manipulated to frustrate the appointment process. The identification of posts is essential and should be pursued earnestly by all establishments.

The court's decision in *Rajeev Prakash Gupta* reinforced the necessity of identifying posts for reservation purposes. Furthermore, a larger bench in the *National Federation of Blind* affirmed this view, establishing a consistent judicial stance that identification under Section 32 must facilitate, not obstruct, the implementation of Section 33. The court emphasised upon the intent of the 1995

8. (2010) 7 SCC 626

9. (2013) 10 SCC 772

10. 2013 SCC OnLine Bom 1547

Act that it is to promote inclusivity and equal opportunity for PwD, and any attempts to frustrate this intent through delays or non-compliance with Section 32 undermine the Act's purpose.

Promotion Denial in the absence of Reservation Provisions for PwD

The core issue addressed by the Supreme Court was whether, in the absence of specific rules for reservation in promotions for PwD, such promotions could be denied. The Appellant State contended that without explicit provisions for reservation in promotion within the rules, PwD should be considered for promotion alongside others in the feeder cadre.

The court emphasised that Section 32 mandates the government to identify posts that can be filled by PwD, which includes posts in the promotional cadre. This identification is a prerequisite for reserving these posts for PwD. The absence of explicit rules for reservation in promotion does not negate the rights of PwD to such reservation, as it is a statutory right flowing from the legislation itself. The court referenced the judgments in *Rajeev Kumar Gupta* and *Siddaraju* cases, which affirm that the absence of rules cannot be used to defeat the legislative intent of providing reservations in promotions for PwD. This ensures that the rights of PwD are upheld even in the absence of specific rules.

The court acknowledged that there might be functional or other legitimate reasons why certain posts in the promotional cadre cannot be reserved for PwD. However, this should not be used as an excuse to undermine the reservation policy. The government must genuinely explore methods to address any resultant stagnation of PwD. The *Amicus Curiae* suggested practical solutions, such as providing promotional opportunities in other departments where posts are identified for PwD or granting higher pay within the same post. These suggestions align with the obligations under Section 47 of the 1995 Act, which mandates reasonable accommodations for PwD.

The court drew parallels with the interpretation of the Rights of Persons with Disabilities Act, 2016 (2016 Act) in *Vikash Kumar v. Union Public Service Commission.*[11] The 2016 Act further strengthens the non-discrimination mandate by requiring 'reasonable accommodation' and ensuring that promotions are not denied merely on the grounds of disability. Defined in Section 2(y) of the 2016 Act, 'reasonable accommodation' includes necessary and appropriate modifications and adjustments to ensure that PwD can enjoy or exercise their rights equally with others. This principle can be applied to interpret and implement the 1995 Act more effectively, ensuring that the legislative intent of providing equal opportunities for PwD is realised.

The Supreme Court's discussion highlights that the absence of explicit rules for reservation in promotions for PwD cannot be a ground to deny such reservations. The legislative mandate, supported by judicial precedents, requires the identification and reservation of promotional posts for PwD. Functional constraints must be addressed through genuine efforts to provide alternative promotional avenues or reasonable accommodations, ensuring that the rights of PwD are protected and promoted in line with both the 1995 and 2016 Acts.

Eligibility for Promotion under PwD Reservation despite Non-Quota Appointment

In addressing whether the Respondent could be promoted under the PwD reservation despite not being initially appointed in the PwD quota, the Supreme Court found this to be a crucial issue justifying

11. (2021) 5 SCC 370

the grant of leave in the SLP. The order by the Kerala High Court directed that the Respondent be considered for promotion based on her disability at the time her claim originally arose, but subject to her seniority relative to other PwD candidates entitled to such reservation. She was also held entitled to notional benefits of her promotion from the date she was found eligible, as discussed above.

The factual context provided by the *Amicus Curiae* highlighted the Respondent's claim for promotion to the post of Upper Division Clerk (UDC) effective from 1 July 2002 and further to the post of Cashier from 20 May 2012. The *Amicus Curiae* sought necessary information from the Appellant State to facilitate the court's understanding. It was pointed out that the Ministry of Social Justice and Empowerment, through the Department of Empowerment of Persons with Disabilities, had identified posts that can be reserved for PwD, including UDC/Cashier. This comprehensive exercise confirmed that the Respondent could discharge the functions of the promotional post, validating her entitlement to the benefit of reservation, even if the rules did not explicitly provide for reservation in promotion. This interpretation aligns with the legislative mandate of Section 32 of the 1995 Act, intended to facilitate, not impede, reservations for PwD.

Regarding the Respondent not being initially appointed under the PwD quota in the feeder cadre, the court noted no dispute about her benchmark disability. It observed that it would be discriminatory and against the constitutional mandate to deny her promotion in the PwD quota based on this technicality. Once appointed, she should be considered on equal footing with other PwD cadre members. The court highlighted an apparent anomaly: if entry point determined eligibility, a person who became disabled after joining service through the normal recruitment process would similarly be ineligible for promotion to a post reserved for PwD. This outcome is illogical and contradicts the legislative intent.

The 1995 Act does not differentiate between those who entered service due to disability and those who acquired disability during service. Similarly, individuals entering service through compassionate appointments should not face discriminatory promotion practices based on their mode of entry. The court's stance reinforces that the source of recruitment should not influence promotion eligibility; what matters is the employee's disability status at the time of promotion consideration. This interpretation ensures non-discrimination and upholds the rights of PwD as envisioned by the 1995 Act. In furtherance to the above discussion, the Supreme Court upheld the High Court's order, emphasising the necessity of implementing reservation in promotion for PwD as mandated by the judgments in the *Rajeev Kumar Gupta* and *Siddaraju* cases. The court directed the State of Kerala to identify and reserve all relevant posts within three months, ensuring compliance with the 1995 Act.

Conclusion

The judgment in *Leesamma Joseph* represents a significant advancement in the broader context of disability rights and affirmative action in India. By addressing the critical issue of reservation in promotions for PwD, the Supreme Court of India's decision reinforces the legislative intent of the 1995 Act. The court held that the absence of specific provisions for reservation in promotion in the service rules does not negate the right of PwD to such reservations. This ruling mandates the identification of posts that can be reserved for PwD, ensuring that administrative delays and non-compliance do not become tools to deny PwD their rightful opportunities. Furthermore, the judgment emphasises that a PwD should be considered for promotion irrespective of whether they were initially appointed under the PwD quota, thus reinforcing the principle of equality and preventing discrimination against individuals who acquire a disability after joining the service.

The judgment, which was also cited by the Supreme Court in subsequent rulings, emphasises the necessity for continuous legislative and policy reforms to address emerging challenges and ensure the protection of the rights of PwD. The judgment has been referenced in other important cases, including *Reserve Bank of India v. A.K. Nair,*[12] to stress upon the importance of reservation in promotions for PwD and the need for proactive measures to ensure equal opportunities for career progression. By placing this judgment within the broader context of disability rights, it is evident that while legislative frameworks are essential, their effective implementation is crucial for achieving true inclusivity and equality for PwD in India.

12. 2023 SCC OnLine SC 801

Raj Kumar Makkad & Himani Makkad

Raj Kumar Makkad is a lawyer with a distinguished career spanning three decades in the legal profession. Holding BCom and LLB degrees, he has served in various important legal and administrative roles, significantly contributing to the legal landscape of Haryana. He, as a former State Commissioner for Persons with Disabilities, Haryana, has been honoured with a National Award from the President of India for his exemplary work where he played a pivotal role in implementing the RPwD Act, 2016. His tenure saw over 2000 cases adjudicated and the creation of more than 15,000 new posts for PwD in Haryana.

Mr Makkad's professional journey includes serving as the Deputy Advocate General for the Government of Haryana, handling a vast array of civil and criminal matters. His extensive experience is complemented by his role as a panel lawyer for multiple government and educational institutions, and as a Professor of

Practice at Chandigarh University. He is also prominent at the online legal platform Lawyers Club India.

In addition to his legal practice, Mr Makkad is dedicated to social causes, particularly the Rights of Persons with Disabilities. He has conducted over 1,200 seminars and awareness camps, both nationally and internationally, including on invitation by UNESCO (United Nations Educational, Scientific and Cultural Organization) to speak on the challenges and legal remedies for Persons with Disabilities. His contributions extend to providing free legal consultations to individuals with disabilities, ensuring accessibility in public buildings, and advocating for the employment and rights of PwD.

Himani Makkad is a legal professional with a robust academic background and diverse work experience. She holds an LLM (IP) from Jindal Global Law School, Sonipat, and BBA LLB (IP Hons) from the Institute of Law, Nirma University, Ahmedabad, from where she graduated.

Himani's professional journey began with Sim and San, Attorneys at Law, where she gained initial experience in litigation and Intellectual Property Law. She further advanced her career with RNA IP Attorneys in Gurugram, dealing with trademark and copyright infringement cases. As a legal consultant at the Health Department of Haryana, she focused on service laws and the Haryana Civil Services Rules, drafting legal documents and assisting in disciplinary proceedings. At Shri Vishwakarma Skill University, Gurgaon, she managed in-house legal matters. Currently, as a Senior Associate at JusIP in Chandigarh, Himani works extensively on service matters, with a particular emphasis on disability laws and the Rights of Persons with Disabilities, and also handles litigation, enforcement, and advisory on Intellectual Property matters and commercial disputes, regularly appearing before various legal forums, including the Punjab and Haryana High Court.

In addition to her professional roles, Himani has published research articles and case comments in reputed legal journals. She has completed certifications in Intellectual Property and legal drafting and participated in national seminars and workshops, demonstrating her commitment to continuous learning and professional development.

The Right to Education from the Child's Perspective, a Mirage? An Existential Grey Zone?

Rajneesh Kumar Pandey v. Union of India

Shabnam Aggarwal

> I want to study. I want to learn and do well like my friends. I go to school every day, but my teacher tells me I cannot understand anything and cannot learn. She tells me that I should come to school only on Fridays when the special educator comes. I do not want to sit at home; I want to be with other children in school. The special educator sits with me and other children with disabilities in the resource room, but she does not teach me what is taught in Class. I insist on going to school every day but am ignored by the teacher for most part of the day, and the only time she notices me, she 'reminds' me about my inability to learn. From my heart, I want to tell her that I can learn and do well; just teach me in ways that facilitate my learning.
>
> —*Anish*[1]

1. Literal translation of what is stated by Anish (name changed) as a young child with disability, studying in Grade 3

Anish echoes the voice of countless children with disabilities who face challenges in accessing their Right to Education, yet remain invisible. The Right to Education is extended to children with disabilities both through a general law – The Right to Education Act, 2009 (RTE) and through a special law – The Rights of Persons with Disabilities Act, 2016 (RPwD). Besides these legislative provisions, schemes such as the *Samagra Shiksha* and the National Educational Policy 2020 (NEP) acknowledge the unique needs and concerns of children with disabilities with regard to their education. Yet, children with disabilities remain nobody's babies, with no one taking complete ownership of their education.

The educational landscape for children with disabilities remains fragmented across the Ministries of Education and Social Justice & Empowerment, across the teachers and special educators in charge of their education, and across the laws, policies, and schemes governing their rights. There are enough laws, policies, and schemes addressing the Right to Education of children with disabilities, but they seem to be talking in different voices, making the journey difficult for such children and their families.

When we begin to view the issue from different perspectives, that of special educators or the perspective of the law and policy initiatives, the issue gets further fragmented. We begin to view parts, forgetting to look at it in its entirety. In this process, what tends to be forgotten is the very child with disability for whom the right exists. Without paying heed to the child's perspective, we will not even begin to understand the challenges confronting them.

It is only when we start hearing and acknowledging the voices of children like Anish that we shall get an understanding of the challenges they face and the sense of helplessness and frustration they experience seeing their dreams of education lying shattered, even before they can take off. This, of course, is primarily because of the lack of support systems that ought to be in place and are mandated by law to enable their access to Right to Education.

It is with respect to one of the supports that the system does offer to children with disabilities, that of special educators,[2] a cadre of professionals that was created to work with them and address disability-specific needs and concerns, including education, that the present judgment under discussion deals with. To address the issue of educating children with disabilities through the appointment of special educators, a writ petition, *Rajneesh Kumar Pandey and Others v. Union of India,*[3] was filed in the Supreme Court of India. Special educators have long faced challenges in getting recognised as an integral part of the system. Representing both the special educators possessing a degree in Special Education and those holding a diploma, the Petitioner sought relief for special educators from the court.

The Plea

The Petitioner brought to the attention of the court the 'illegality being committed by the State and its authorities in employing them in recognised schools on a contract basis without any certainty of tenure.'[4] The writ petition emphasised that there was an 'obligation of the State to ensure that the pupil-teacher ratio is maintained in the recognised schools, by appointing an adequate number of trained teachers on regular posts.'[5] The court had before

2. Special educators have to be trained and registered with the Rehabilitation Council of India (RCI) under the RCI (Rehabilitation Council of India) Act, 1992

3. (2021) 17 SCC 1

4. *Id.*, para 1

5. *Id.*, para 2

it another writ petition[6] tagged with *Rajneesh Kumar Pandey's* case, raising similar issues with respect to the employment of special educators. The Petitioners sought directions from the court for the appointment of special educators on the basis of a Pupil-Teacher Ratio (PTR) of 5:1. The Petitioners drew attention to the fact that special educators were employed in schools on a contractual basis, without any certainty of tenure. They wanted the government to reserve at least two posts or a minimum number of posts, as deemed fit by the court, in each and every school across the country and reserve a minimum number of posts in every pending vacancy and future vacancy of teachers in schools, across the country, aided by the State as well as the Central Government.

The 2017 Petition, besides raising the points mentioned above, sought directions from the court for the creation of over seventy thousand posts of special education teachers in the State of Uttar Pradesh and close to twenty thousand posts in Punjab for fulfilling the 5:1 PTR for children with disabilities.

The Court's View

On the core issue of PTR, the court noted that PTR was detailed in the Schedule of the RTE Act,[7] and Rule 22 of the RTE states that the PTR is to be notified by the Central Government or other appropriate government. However, the court went on to state that in the absence of norms and standards for the appointment of teachers for children with disabilities and the ratio to be maintained, 'the provisions of the special law governing the Rights of Persons with Disabilities or the schemes formulated by the executive, in that

6. The second tagged petition was Writ Petition (Civil) No. 876 of 2017

7. Right to Education Act 2009, The Schedule (under Section 19)

regard, must come into play.'[8] The court also noted that while the Schedule did not make any distinction between general and special schools, the norms specified therein for general schools cannot be replicated in special schools, which are governed by special laws.

The court stated that the Central Government must issue a notification laying down the ratio, 'a minimum benchmark' for the appointment of special educators in general and special schools. These norms, eventually notified in 2022, determined a PTR of 10:1 for grades (classes) 1 to 5 and 15:1 for grades 6 to 8; and stated that the 'one special educator per school' norm would remain intact and that special educators would operate in itinerant mode in special circumstances.

The court directed that until norms for PTR for children with disabilities were put in place, those ascertained in the *Reshma Parveen*[9] order should serve as a stopgap arrangement. The norms laid down a PTR of 8:1 for children with cerebral palsy, 5:1 for children with intellectual disability, ASD, and specific learning disabilities, and 2:1 for deaf-blind and a combination of two or more of the seven disabilities mentioned.[10]

Among the many observations made by the court, one that stands out and seems to reflect the court's perspective is when it states, reproducing an earlier interim order passed in the same matter,

> We are of the prima facie view that the children with special needs have to be imparted education not only by special teachers but there have to be special schools for them…It is impossible to think that the children who are disabled

8. *Supra* note 3, para 37

9. *Reshma Parveen v. Directorate of Education, State (NCT of Delhi)*, Case no. 82/1014/2019/04/9072-84. Order Dated 31 December 2019 (State Commissioner for Persons with Disabilities)

10. *Supra* note 3, para 67

> or suffer from any kind of disability or who are mentally challenged can be included in the mainstream schools for getting education.[11]

The court clarified that by disability, it meant 'the students who suffer from blindness, deafness, and autism or such types of disorder may be required to have separate schools with distinctly trained teachers.'[12]

The court seems to suggest that special schools are the most suitable places for children with disabilities, especially the three groups of children specifically mentioned, and education cannot be imparted to them in a mainstream school. This observation, however, at many levels might be at odds with the principle of inclusive education that is woven through our laws. While special schools remain an integral part of the lives of children with disabilities and play an important role, they remain one of the many avenues open for them. Many students with disabilities who have traversed the general education system and gone on to pursue higher education stand testimony to the fact that inclusion works for them. An inclusive education system is what our laws also speak about, though with varying undertones.

The Legal and Policy Statement

Article 21A of the Constitution of India made education a Fundamental Right, and the RTE Act, 2009, extended the Right to Education to all children in the six to fourteen year age group. Through an amendment in 2012, children with disabilities were explicitly brought under its fold, and with it came the right to be included in mainstream schools. For children with high support

11. *Id,* para 6

12. *Ibid.*

needs,[13] it offered a choice of home-based education. Barring home-based education, which remained a contentious issue due to its ad-hoc nature, the Act provided an impetus for children to be enrolled in mainstream schools.

The RPwD Act 2016 channeled the rights enshrined in the UN Convention into legal rights. The 'people first' perspective brought a new way of thinking and reignited the hope for change. It extended the Right to Education to all children aged 6 to 18 years,[14] and defined inclusive education[15] as 'a system of education wherein students with and without disability learn together, and the system of teaching and learning is suitably adapted to meet the learning needs of different types of students with disabilities.' In the midst of the positive steps towards endeavouring to provide inclusive education, it also offered the option of a special school.[16]

A Right Diluted

The RTE Act, the RPwD Act, together with the NEP 2020, offer a bouquet of 'choices' – of studying in mainstream schools, in special schools, through the Open School system, or in the home-based education system, leaving it to the parents to decide the best option for their child. By opening up the options, the Right to Education has been diluted. Diluted because we seem to be drifting away from our commitment to inclusive education. This has also resulted in mainstream schools trying to evade responsibility by taking the plea that they do not have the systems in place or do not have a special educator for teaching children with disabilities.

---

13. Earlier referred to as children with 'severe' disability

14. RPwD Act 2016, Section 31(i)

15. *Id.*, Section 2(m)

16. *Id.*, Section 31(1)

The mainstream school system can only be strengthened to extend quality education to all children when there is a firm commitment towards inclusion. When diversions are created and other 'choices' are offered, the thrust towards seeing all children through the lens of diversity and including them in mainstream schools is lost.

There are enough good practices across the country to showcase the fact that children, regardless of disability, can attend mainstream schools, can learn with their peers, and even excel in their chosen fields. The life journey of Srikant Bolla,[17] a person with vision impairment, making it to MIT and now a successful businessman, is a case in point. To enable their education, all that children with disabilities need is to be included in a class and learn with access to all necessary individual supports and reasonable accommodations incorporated within their legal Right to Education. These include access to physical spaces, access to information, teaching-learning material, aids, appliances, and devices; opportunities to participate in sports, co-curricular activities, and other supports that enable the child with a disability to function on an equal basis with their peers. Section 16 of the RPwD Act is all-encompassing and spells out the responsibility of the government to ensure that children can receive education in an inclusive set-up. The need of the hour is to direct efforts toward strengthening the mainstream system of education rather than vacillating between the two systems and losing the momentum that was just starting to build.

While mainstream education is crucial, special schools play a vital role in equipping children with disabilities for independent

17. *Times of India*, 'TOI Dialogues Kanpur: "Man of Paper" Srikanth Bolla shares insights on resilience and his "success mantra"' (23 September 2024), available at: https://timesofindia.indiatimes.com/toi-dialogues/toi-dialogues-kanpur-man-of-paper-srikanth-bolla-shares-insights-on-resilience-and-his-success-mantra/articleshow/113607914.cms (accessed 11 December 2024)

living. Though often seen as separate systems, special and mainstream schools exist on the same continuum. Special schools provide specialised resources, trained educators, and tailored support, serving as stepping-stones for mainstream inclusion. Many children, especially those with high support needs, continue in special schools due to their specific accommodations. However, these schools fall under the Department of Empowerment of Persons with Disabilities rather than the Ministry of Education. While some align with formal education systems, others use independent curricula, often leaving students without recognised certification. Furthermore, no equivalent special spaces exist in higher education, making school-level inclusion essential for a smoother academic transition.

Efforts have been made to integrate special and mainstream schools by positioning special schools as resource centres and supporting teachers with strategies and materials for better disability-inclusive education. Greater synergy between both systems is needed for holistic learning and improved outcomes. Currently, special educators serve as the bridge, teaching in both settings, but they continue to face their own challenges, as highlighted in the present discussion.

Many-a-Gap: Absence of a Sufficient Number of Special Educators

As stated in the earlier part of this chapter, two specific issues raised in the petition were the appointment of two special educators on a regular basis in every school and of maintaining a PTR of 5:1.

Here, data becomes important to contextualise the situation and help make the invisible visible and more tangible. There are 26.52 crore children studying in 14.89 lakh schools, taught by 95 lakh teachers across the country. There are 18,41,995 children with disabilities enrolled in government schools across the country, enrolled in grades 1 to 8.[18] There would be many more in kindergarten and in senior school. Add to this children with disabilities who are enrolled in private schools and special schools across the country. Contrasted with the 1,35,643[19] registered special educators available in the country, the feasibility of meeting PTR norms seems remote. The response to an RTI (Right to Information) application in Punjab revealed that one special educator oversees 150 children with disabilities on average, and even up to 300 in some smaller and border towns.[20]

Special educators cannot replace subject teachers, as their training does not equip them to teach across disabilities, grades, or curricula. Their role is better suited to adapting curricula, providing accessible learning materials, and supporting children and parents with resources and government linkages. However, without a defined job profile, they are often expected to take on unrealistic responsibilities.

One real example is an educator managing 90 children across 40 geographically dispersed schools, meeting each only once or twice a month. She tirelessly navigates challenging terrain, working year-round, including a summer program requiring daily

---

18. Ministry of Education, 'Report on Unified District Information System For Education Plus (UDISE+) 2021–22 Flash Statistics' (Government of India), available at: https://udiseplus.gov.in/#/en/page/publications (accessed 12 December 2024)

19. In response to a question raised in the Lok Sabha, the RCI said that 1,35,643 special educators serving in disability sector were registered, as on 24.03.2022, in the Central Rehabilitation Register. Ministry of Social Justice and Empowerment, 'Teachers for Disabled' (Government of India), available at: https://sansad.in/getFile/loksabhaquestions/annex/178/AU4235.pdf?source=pqals (accessed 12 December 2024)

20. Divya Goyal, 'Just one teacher for every 150 children with special needs in Punjab, reveals RTI' (*The Indian Express,* 28 July 2024), available at: https://indianexpress.com/article/cities/chandigarh/punjab-teachers-rte-students-rti-9478369/ (accessed 13 December 2024)

home visits to 44 children—failure results in salary loss. Despite 15 years of experience, she earns only ₹14,000 per month and remains on a contractual basis, highlighting the precarity of her profession.

Sanjana, a special educator in a primary school, holds a regular post with a standard salary. However, due to teacher shortage, she also serves as the Grade 3 class teacher. As the only special educator, she has identified 12 children with disabilities across grades, all assigned to her class. Balancing their needs with the rest of the students, she struggles to provide adequate attention, leaving these children technically enrolled but overlooked.

These cases highlight the impracticality of a uniform 10:1 PTR. With education on the Concurrent List, States have the autonomy to set policies, leading to vast disparities that make standardisation challenging.

What needs to be Done to Actualise the Rights of the Child?

Time for systemic change

Despite progress, children with disabilities are still far from fully realising their Right to Education. A truly inclusive system remains elusive, and fragmented efforts do more harm than good. The entire education framework needs urgent reform to ensure readiness for inclusive, quality education. Reasonable accommodation,[21] as mandated by the RPwD Act, must be embedded in the system to make education a genuine right for all children with disabilities. Until seamless access to such accommodations is ensured, their educational journey will remain fraught with obstacles.

21. RPwD Act 2016, Section 2(y)

Evolving a Multi-pronged strategy

Achieving true inclusion and quality education for children with disabilities requires a multi-pronged strategy. With a shortage of special educators and ideal PTRs unattainable in the near future, mainstream teachers must be better trained for inclusive teaching. Special educators should be reimagined as key resource professionals, collaborating with teachers to assess individual needs, provide necessary support, and bridge learning gaps. Strengthening their training to offer cross-disability support is essential to ensuring every child learns to their full potential alongside peers.

A Child-first and Child-centric Approach

Amidst these challenges, the dreams of lakhs of children with disabilities often go unnoticed. They long to attend school, learn alongside their peers, and build a future for themselves—however small their niche in the world may be. Like everyone else, they aspire to independence, employment, and the freedom to shape their lives. But for these aspirations to become reality, access to quality education remains the essential first step.

Shift the Onus

The journey of securing education for children with disabilities is fraught with challenges, leaving many parents exhausted from fighting for their children's rights. Poverty and disability are deeply interconnected, making survival itself a struggle—one that should not include the battle for education. Many give up, especially when, despite their efforts, their child is still excluded from the classroom.

The responsibility lies with all of us to ensure that legal provisions are implemented without forcing children, parents, and professionals to fight for rights that are already theirs. While an ideal PTR remains distant, we cannot afford endless delays. The system must be strong enough to prioritise the child's perspective—because a child with a disability is, first and foremost, a child. A firm commitment to every child's right to education must drive the necessary accommodations and support.

Laws, policies, and schemes exist, but their impact depends on the will to enforce them. In navigating different educational models and approaches, the child must remain at the centre. Delays in reform may seem like a matter of years to us, but for these children, it is their only childhood—one that will not return. We must hold ourselves accountable for a generation of children with disabilities who, despite having a Right to Education, remain on the margins or outside the system entirely. Too many drop out, not by choice, but due to a system that fails to meet their needs. Others, like Anish, attend school yet receive no education.

The day children like Anish begin questioning why education remains out of reach for them, we will have no answers—only the painful truth that we have failed them.

Shabnam Aggarwal

Shabnam Aggarwal's area of specialisation pertains to disability. She has been working in this field for over thirty years. Her formal training includes an MA in Psychology, a Certificate course and training in Specific Learning Disability (Dyslexia) and Counselling, a BEd in Special Education, and a degree in Law. These trainings have enabled her integrate various perspectives and concerns in her work.

As the Founder Director of *Anandini*, a registered society that focuses on disability advocacy, research, and training, she supports the Rights of Persons with Disabilities.

Her work experience spans across disability, from working with children with Specific Learning Disability, specifically Dyslexia, to children and persons with high support needs, such as cerebral palsy, intellectual and other disabilities, their families, and other stakeholders, understanding and supporting their various needs and concerns.

She has been conducting training workshops in schools, Government and Non-Government Organisations for parents, professionals, CBR (Community-Based Rehabilitation) workers, special educators, and school principals. These sessions have been conducted on learning disability, developmental disabilities, and other specific conditions, on laws and legal Rights of Persons with Disabilities, and the UN Convention on the Rights of Persons with Disabilities. The sessions support teachers in creating inclusive classrooms and spaces through the use of effective teaching strategies and assistive technology. Sharing of experiences and journeys of children helps them view things through the lens of the child and understand their perspective.

The other facet of her work has been conducting research, impact assessments, and creating and writing training modules, reports, and related documents. The research studies and advocacy initiatives that she has been involved with have been in areas that directly impact children and Persons with Disabilities and their families, focusing on the Right to Education, Child Protection, and Assisted Living. These studies provide an insight into lived experiences. Information from Persons with Disabilities and their families and other key stakeholders is collated and viewed through the lens of the law and policy framework. These create a platform for discussion, debate, and advocacy for policy change directed toward improving access to rights for children and Persons with Disabilities.

A Glimmer of Hope

Vikash Kumar v. Union Public Service Commission

Srianusha Thotakura & Apoorva Pushkarna

In 2017, Vikash Kumar, a young medical graduate, had been preparing for the Civil Services Examination with the aspiration of becoming an officer with the Government of India. Pursuant to this goal, he reached out to the examiners, requesting the assistance of a scribe to appear for the examination in light of his locomotor disability. However, the examiners refused to provide a scribe, deeming his disability insufficient to qualify for a scribe. Despite multiple attempts to secure such assistance, he was unable to convince them of his need. In a helpless state, he finally knocked on the doors of the court, seeking judicial intervention. This led to a long legal battle, which ultimately reached the Supreme Court of India.

Vikash's story is one among many cases where crucial support has been denied to those facing barriers in education, employment, or other public services. Vikash's determination and perseverance paved the way for the landmark judgment in *Vikash Kumar v. Union Public Service Commission*[1] in 2021. Although initiated in

1. (2021) 5 SCC 370

hopes of finding a solution for the scribe issue, the apex court did far more than treat it as an individual grievance. The court took this opportunity to clarify the scope of some significant disability rights related to the Rights of Persons with Disabilities Act, 2016. The judgment not only extensively highlighted some of the most important rights provided in the Act for the inclusion of the disabled in different aspects of society but also shed light on the intention behind legislating such provisions. Today, the case is celebrated for its progressive stance and has proven to be a ray of hope for many in similar situations.

This chapter delves into the significance of the judgment in the evolution of disability rights jurisprudence in India and its larger implications for Persons with Disabilities (PwD). It particularly examines the important concepts and principles related to disability rights discussed in the case.

The Background

Vikash Kumar, the Appellant in the case, was a young medical graduate who aspired to serve the government. In 2017, he applied to write the Civil Services Examination conducted by the Union Public Service Commission (UPSC) to achieve this goal. However, he had a neurological condition, dysgraphia (commonly known as writer's cramp), which impacts the ability to use one's hands. Due to the locomotor disability caused by his condition, Vikash requested the UPSC to provide him with the service of a scribe for the examination. To his dismay, his request was denied. The UPSC reasoned that based on their examination rules, only candidates with blindness, cerebral palsy, or locomotor disabilities of not less than 40% were eligible to a scribe. It was determined that the Appellant's disability at 6% was not a benchmark disability. The qualifying criterion of a benchmark disability is that the disability is more than 40%. Aggrieved by this need to meet the set stringent threshold, Vikash approached the justice system for resolution. Following extended litigation, he finally approached the Supreme Court of India, seeking redressal.

Paving an Inclusive Path

When Vikash approached the Supreme Court, the judges did not merely treat the case as an individual issue. Rather, they went a step ahead to clarify the scope of certain key provisions of the Rights of Persons with Disabilities Act, 2016 (the Act). They undertook this exercise in the interest of the larger community of Persons with Disabilities, attempting to provide direction to all those who traverse a similar path. The court repeatedly highlighted the social welfare focus of the Act as it engaged with the key issues of the case and clarified the scope of some provisions of the Act. Furthermore, the court explained how the rights available to Persons with Disabilities stem from the fundamental guarantees afforded by the Constitution of India.

The Constitutional Rights and Freedoms

The Constitution of India grants certain basic rights to every person in India, called the fundamental rights. There are three articles, collectively called the 'Golden Triangle', which guarantee these essential rights – Articles 14, 15, and 21. Article 14 of the Constitution of India, 1950, provides the right to equality and equal protection under the law, casting a duty on the State to treat every individual in the same manner, regardless of their background. Article 15 provides the right against discrimination, ensuring that every person has equal access to public places and services. Finally, Article 21 guarantees the fundamental right to life and personal liberty, setting out that every person should be able to enjoy a life of dignity and freedom.

Furthermore, it has been recognised in the Constitution that equality is grounded in two principles that go hand in hand: non-discrimination and reasonable differentiation. These two principles cast negative as well as positive obligations on the State. Firstly, the State is tasked with the duty of eliminating all instances of discrimination wherein persons are denied equal rights and freedoms without any reasonable and just cause. Secondly, it is emphasised that it is simultaneously essential to uproot the deep-seated structural issues by taking specific measures. These specific measures are particularly important for uplifting the disadvantaged groups and bringing them on par with the privileged groups. For this purpose, it is permissible for such disadvantaged groups to be treated differently from the privileged groups and afforded certain rights and protections to ultimately bring them on a level playing field.[2]

The Rights of Persons with Disabilities Act, 2016

Pursuant to the rights, freedoms, and liberties promised by the Indian Constitution, particularly the 'Golden Triangle' and International Conventions, India legislated the Rights of Persons with Disabilities Act, 2016. This Act is heavily grounded in the principles of equality and non-discrimination. In pursuit of these principles, the Act primarily casts two broader duties on the State. First, to ensure that no person with a disability is subjected to any form of discrimination. Second, an affirmative duty to ensure that all PwD enjoy the 'right to equality, a life of dignity and respect for their integrity on par with others'.[3]

2. The Constitution of India, 1950, Articles 14 and 15

3. The RPD Act, 2016, Section 3(1)

The Act clearly states that government establishments cannot discriminate against PwD[4] and clarifies that the private sector is also not allowed to discriminate against PwD.[5] The Act obligates the provision of reasonable accommodations to all PwD.[6] Under the Act, there is a distinction made between Section 2(r):

> 'person with benchmark disability' means a person with not less than 40% of a specified disability, where specified disability has not been defined in measurable terms, and includes a person with disability where specified disability has been defined in measurable terms, as certified by the certifying authority.[7]

and Section 2(s):

> 'person with disability' means a person with long-term physical, mental, intellectual, or sensory impairment which, in interaction with barriers, hinders his full and effective participation in society equally with others.[8]

This distinction is significant because persons with benchmark disabilities who have more than 40% of a specified disability may require special support as outlined in the Act such as resverations. Meanwhile, the broader category of Persons with Disabilities includes all individuals with disabilities, regardless of the extent and type of their impairments. This inclusive approach ensures

4. *Id.,* Section 2(h)
5. *Id.*, Rules
6. *Id.*, Section 20
7. *Id.*, Section 2(r)
8. *Id.*, Section 2(s)

that a wide range of disabilities is recognised and that necessary accommodations and supports are provided to enable full participation in society.

The Act also details various rights and entitlements for PwD, such as access to education, employment, and social security. It emphasises the need to create an inclusive environment through accessible physical infrastructure, transportation, information, and communication technologies. By integrating these provisions, the Act's overall aim and objective is to eliminate the barriers faced by PwD and promote their full inclusion and participation in all aspects of life.

In summary, the Rights of Persons with Disabilities Act, 2016, is a comprehensive piece of legislation that addresses the rights and needs of PwD in India. It reinforces the principles of equality and non-discrimination and seeks to create an inclusive society by providing necessary accommodations and support to PwD, ensuring their full and effective participation in all spheres of life.

The Judgment

Coming back to the case at hand, the court expressed its disappointment regarding the policy divide within the two bodies, UPSC and the Ministry of Social Justice and Empowerment (MSJE). While the UPSC, responsible for setting the rules pertaining to the civil services examination, had been stringent and had adamantly allowed only persons with benchmark disabilities to avail the services of the scribe, MSJE, responsible for implementing the provisions of the RPwD Act, was more flexible and allowed for the inclusion of non-benchmark disabilities for the purposes of providing a scribe. This discord and lack of uniformity were frowned upon as it seemed to be in contravention of the interest of Persons with Disabilities.

The court further touched upon the distinction between the phrases 'Persons with Disabilities' as used in Section 2(s) of the Act and 'Persons with Benchmark Disabilities' as used in Section 2(r) of the Act. The phrase 'Persons with Disabilities' was clarified as an umbrella term. It included both persons with benchmark disabilities and those without benchmark disabilities. It was observed that the provisions are applicable to both categories of Persons with Disabilities as long as it is mentioned as 'Persons with Disabilities'. The provisions that explicitly target persons with benchmark disabilities are clearly delineated within the Act. There are two specific chapters in the Act, Chapters VI and VII, dedicated to persons with benchmark disabilities. There are certain extra protections and provisions for this category of persons such as free education and reservations, as they are more vulnerable owing to the extent/nature of their disability and might often require more support or assistance. Therefore, it can be interpreted that the phrase 'Persons with Disabilities' includes the entire disability community, including persons without benchmark disabilities.

The Act clearly provides for the provision of reasonable accommodations to PwD. The provisions of the Act, however, nowhere explicitly mention that reasonable accommodations would only be provided to persons with benchmark disabilities. The court also looked at the purpose of the Act while interpreting the scope of the provision of reasonable accommodation for more clarity on the matter. Sensing that the Act had been promulgated for the empowerment and welfare of the larger disabled community, it was deemed unlikely that the legislature had intended only for persons with benchmark disabilities to seek reasonable accommodations. Hence, it was held that it was erroneous to assume that reasonable accommodations should only be provided to persons with benchmark disabilities, as this assumption goes against the two cardinal principles of non-discrimination and reasonable differentiation enshrined in the Constitution of India, which are required to be applied when taking a holistic view of the provisions of the Act.

Lastly, the court elaborated on the principle of reasonable accommodations. '*Reasonable Accommodations*' refer to individualised adjustments or adaptations made to meet the specific needs of individuals with disabilities, effectively removing barriers that hinder their participation in societal functions such as education, employment, and general enjoyment of life. These accommodations are tailored to recognise and address the unique challenges faced by each individual. For example, a reasonable accommodation for an employee with a hearing impairment could include providing a sign-language interpreter, speech-to-text conversion software, or closed captions on all audio content. Similarly, for an employee with a locomotor disability, reasonable accommodation might involve the option to work from home, adjustments in seating arrangements, or making the desk wheelchair accessible. These measures ensure that individuals with disabilities can perform tasks and participate in activities on an equal footing with others, promoting inclusivity and equal opportunity.

Keeping all these factors in mind, the Supreme Court's decision in the case explained that the statute of the Rights of Persons with Disabilities Act, 2016, had been enacted with the aim of empowering PwD. Disallowing a candidate from seeking the assistance of a scribe was in contravention of the aim and overall objective of the Act. Disallowing a person with a disability from availing the scribe assistance, which was required to put that person at par with their companions taking the exam, was being seen as not only causing hindrance in the act of writing (an action necessary for taking the exam) but also rendering the person at a disadvantage compared to the able-bodied peers. This was seen as a form of discrimination. Therefore, the court allowed Vikash Kumar, the Appellant, to seek the assistance of a scribe. The court further passed directions that the Ministry of Social Justice and Empowerment should draft rules in such a manner that they are not discriminatory and enable PwD to perform at an equal level as others.

Reflections

Several judgments over the years have made it clear that the objective of disability-related laws that empower PwD is to enable them to 'live a life of purpose and human dignity'. The courts have liberally interpreted various provisions to favour PwD and have reiterated that legislation with respect to PwD is a beneficial social legislation. The provisions should not be construed in a strictly technical and apathetic manner. If the legislature has made provisions for reservations for PwD, it can be interpreted that PwD are deemed capable of performing tasks at par with persons without disabilities. It is imperative to ensure accessibility and provide reasonable accommodations to enable PwD to discharge their duties and participate equally. It is sufficient to prove that the person is not hindered by their disability from carrying out their responsibilities efficiently and is not prejudicing the interests of other stakeholders.[9] Hence, a hyper-technical and mechanical approach is not desirable in a welfare state like India.

Conclusion

While the *Vikash Kumar* case is a monumental judgment in Indian legal history, aiming to broaden the scope of reasonable accommodation and disability rights, it inadvertently overlooks the bureaucratic hurdles that Persons with Disabilities face. The apex court recognised the social inequalities that set back

9. *Syed Bashir-ud-din Qadri v. Nazir Ahmed Shah and Others*, (2010) 3 SCC 603

Persons with Disabilities but ultimately fell into the same trap of bureaucratic oversight by delegating the responsibility of drafting 'proper' guidelines for the issuance of scribes in examinations to the Ministry of Social Justice and Empowerment. However, it inadvertently places the autonomy of PwD in the hands of external entities rather than empowering the individuals themselves, again leaving them at the mercy of interpretation or subjective analysis by official agencies.

In attempting to streamline the process and ensure fairness, the court's directive to the Ministry may perpetuate delays and obstacles inherent in bureaucratic systems. The official systems often lack the agility and responsiveness needed to address the immediate and unique needs of individuals with disabilities. As a result, the Supreme Court's decision, while so well-intentioned, risks entangling individuals in further red tape, thereby undermining the very rights it seeks to protect. Moreover, there is always an added external factor of proper representation of the disabled community on the boards of makers of such guidelines/rules and policies, which can dilute the personal agency of PwD. It shifts the decision-making power away from those who are directly affected and places it in the hands of those who may not fully understand or prioritise the nuanced needs of the disabled community. This approach has almost always led to generic, one-size-fits-all solutions that fail to adequately address individual requirements, which again hits at the core and weakens the idea of granting free and fair disability rights to PwD, which might require an individualised approach on a person-to-person basis.

Nonetheless, the judgment has had a significant impact on the community and its understanding of disability. The progressive attitude and influence of the judgment are evident in various subsequent rulings on disability rights. This case has not only brought the understanding of the judicial system towards recognising the broader ambit of the Act but has also moved beyond the legislation to consider all forms of disabilities faced by individuals. The effect on other courts in the hierarchy has also been noteworthy. For example, in a recent case, the Madras High Court observed, 'All persons having disability have special needs. That does not mean the disabled as defined in the statute alone have special needs.'[10] Beneficial principles and doctrines have to be expansively construed and applied. This approach underscores the importance of removing barriers to create a more equitable society for all. The judgment has also played a key role in furthering the long-standing disability rights movement. It is a notable step forward in addressing the seemingly never-ending challenges faced by the disabled community in India. The judgment impresses upon treating the community with the dignity and respect it deserves. It reminds us that PwD are equally entitled to the fundamental rights of equality and non-discrimination, as guaranteed by the Constitution of India. The principle of reasonable accommodations has been emphasised as a means to achieving these fundamental rights, which are, anyway, guaranteed to us.

The case is particularly relevant as it takes an inclusive approach while interpreting important provisions of the Act. Those with a lesser degree of disability, as well as those with a higher degree, are provided basic rights and freedoms without distinction. The barriers they face are acknowledged as external challenges that need to be remedied through measures such as reasonable accommodations. This judgment is a victory for all those who have been steadfast in their quest for respect and dignity. While it does not remove all barriers that PwD encounter on a daily basis, it certainly paves the path for those who wish to live a life of dignity. The judgment

10. *Monisha v. National Testing Agency*, 2024 SCC OnLine Mad 956

serves as a beacon of hope for many and promises to usher more inclusive legal and policy changes.

Vikash Kumar is a reminder that the fight for disability rights is incessant and requires continuous effort and vigilance. It emphasises the importance of legal protections, policy changes, and societal attitudes in creating a truly inclusive society. As we move forward, it is essential to build on this judgment and continue working towards a world where PwD can fully enjoy their rights and live with dignity and respect.

Srianusha Thotakura & Apoorva Pushkarna

Anusha Thotakura teaches at OP Jindal Global University and is a Research Associate at the Centre for Justice, Law, and Society (CJLS). She holds an LLM degree from the University of California, Berkeley, where she received the Irving Tragen Law School Fellowship and the Logan Scholarship. She also completed her BA LLB (Hons) degree at OP Jindal Global University.

In her role at the university, Anusha is involved in teaching courses such as Labour Law, Natural Resources Law, and Alternative Dispute Resolution.

At CJLS, Anusha focuses on research and advocacy in areas such as sexual and reproductive health and rights, anti-carceral politics, gender and sexuality, and disability rights. Her work includes conducting research, developing policy recommendations, and collaborating with various stakeholders to promote social justice and legal reforms.

Anusha is dedicated to advancing these fields through her academic work and practical engagements.

Apoorva Pushkarna is an Associate at JusIP, specialising in Intellectual Property Rights (IPR). With a BA LLB and an LLM in IPR and Technology from Jindal Global Law School, her expertise spans trademarks, copyright, and domain names, complemented by her proficiency in legal transactional work, particularly in drafting contracts.

Apoorva's litigation practice is notable in both Intellectual Property and Constitutional matters, with significant experience in the High Court of Punjab and Haryana and the Armed Forces Tribunal.

Beyond her legal practice, Apoorva is a passionate disability rights activist. Her advocacy began during her college days, focusing on creating a more inclusive and equitable society for Persons with Disabilities, and also dealing with cases of disabled soldiers in Armed Forces Tribunal.

Uncovering and Dislodging the Constructedness of Structural Ableism

Disabled Rights Group v. Union of India

Jaideep Singh Lalli & Ananya Sharma

On 15 December 2017, the Supreme Court of India delivered a landmark decision in *Disabled Rights Group v. Union of India,*[1] ordering all educational institutions run or aided by the Government to honour their obligation to reserve 5% seats for Persons with Disabilities and to report their compliance to the authorities established under the Rights of Persons with Disabilities Act 2016. In addition, the court directed the formation of a committee to recommend ways to make educational institutions' physical spaces and pedagogical practices accessible to Persons with Disabilities within a given time frame.

This decision came in response to a writ petition filed in 2006 in public interest for the benefit of Persons with Disabilities. Originally filed only in respect of law colleges, the Supreme Court, in its wisdom, decided to extend the coverage of the petition to all educational institutions. By the time the petition was decided with final orders and directions, it had remained pending for eleven long

1. (2018) 2 SCC 397

years. The apex court explained this delay by highlighting that it had been calling for status reports from the Respondent governmental authorities from time to time about the implementation of relevant provisions under the Disabilities Act.

The petition primarily raised three issues. First, the petition highlighted the non-implementation of the obligation to reserve 3% seats for Persons with Disabilities in educational institutions as per Section 39 of the Persons with Disability Act 1995. By the time final orders were passed, the 1995 Act had been replaced by the 2016 Act; this is significant because the 2016 Act requires 5% seats to be reserved for Persons with Disabilities in place of the 3% prescription under the 1995 Act. Second, the petition raised the issue of ensuring that infrastructure and facilities at educational institutions are made accessible for orthopaedically disabled persons. Third, the petition underscored the importance of adapting pedagogical methods to the needs of persons with disability. While synthesising its analysis of applicable legislation with lessons from disability rights theory, the judgment discusses each of the three issues systematically.

Reservation of Seats in Educational Institutions

After setting out the aforementioned context in which the petition arose, the judgment begins by tracing the statutory development that the reservation requirement had undergone between the time when the petition was filed and the time of the final orders. At the time when the petition was filed, Section 39 of the 1995 Act required all governmental educational institutions and those aided by the government to reserve at least 3% seats for Persons with Disabilities. The provision was discussed by the Supreme Court in *All Kerala Parents Association of Hearing Impaired v. State of*

Kerala,[2] where it issued directions requiring all government and educational institutions aided by the government to necessarily comply with Section 39 of the 1995 Act. In that judgment, while quoting this provision, the Supreme Court had clarified that 3% is the minimum requirement and that 'it can be even more than 3%'.

However, by the time the petition was ripe for final orders, the 1995 Act had been replaced by the 2016 Act. The 2016 Act made relatively more comprehensive provisions for providing educational facilities to Persons with Disabilities. In the court's own words, 'Section 31 confers the right to free education upon children with benchmark disabilities who are between the ages of six and 18 years. This provision is made notwithstanding anything contained in the Rights of Children to Free and Compulsory Education Act 2009.' Section 32 makes provisions for a 5% reservation in higher educational institutions run or aided by the government for persons with benchmark disabilities, and Section 34 provides for reservation in employment. Noticeably, the 2016 Act makes these provisions for 'persons with benchmark disabilities', an expression that is defined in Section 2(r) of the 2016 Act as follows: 'person with benchmark disability' means a person with not less than 40% of a specified disability where specified disability has not been defined in measurable terms and includes a person with disability where specified disability has been defined in measurable terms, as certified by the certifying authority.

The grievance of the petitioner in relation to these statutory requirements was that educational institutions were not complying with their obligation to reserve seats. Accordingly, the division bench of Justices A.K. Sikri and Ashok Bhushan directed all educational institutions covered by Section 32 of the 2016 Act to comply with the reservation obligation while making admission

2. (2018) 2 SCC 410

decisions each year. To that end, educational institutions were also directed to submit a list of the number of disabled persons admitted in each course every year to the Chief Commissioner and/or the State Commissioner for Persons with Disabilities (as the case may be). The Chief Commissioner, as well as the State Commissioner(s) appointed as per Chapter XII of the 2016 Act, were also tasked with enquiring whether these educational institutions fulfilled their obligations. The judgment emphasised that appropriate action against defaulting educational institutions had to be initiated under Section 89 of the 2016 Act.

Evidently, the Supreme Court's directions in this case on the reservation requirement reinforced and reiterated the statutory framework already in place, a framework that had been accumulating rust as a result of a lamentable lack of compliance by educational institutions.

Making Educational Institutions More Accessible

The second aspect before the Supreme Court of India in the present case was about accessibility to educational institutions as well as access to specific facilities for Persons with Disabilities. In that regard, the court reiterated its directions in *Rajive Raturi v. Union of India*[3] (delivered coincidentally on the same day as the present decision). In *Rajive Raturi*, the Supreme Court issued detailed directions for ensuring provisions for accessibility to handicapped persons, specifically relating to persons who are visually impaired. In *Rajive Raturi*, the apex court affirmed the right to accessibility as a fundamental right protected by the Constitution of India with the aim of preventing any further legislative or executive obstacles towards its enforcement and realisation. The Supreme Court noted:

3. (2018) 2 SCC 413

> The vitality of the issue of 'Accessibility' vis-à-vis visually disabled persons' right to life can be gauged clearly by this court's judgment in *State of Himachal Pradesh & Anr. v. Umed Ram Sharma & Others*,[4] where the right to life under Article 21 has been held broad enough to incorporate the right to accessibility.[5]

The Supreme Court further observed that an expansive reading of Article 21 of the Constitution covers within its ambit 'skill-enhancing facilities', which are required for disabled persons (here, visually impaired) to go about their day-to-day life without suffering indignity. While discussing the right to dignity in the aforesaid decision, the Supreme Court held that this right is applicable equally to every citizen and with 'much more vigour' in the case of Persons with Disabilities. The Supreme Court observed how the 1995 Act placed a responsibility on the State to ensure that such 'skill-enhancing' facilities were provided by grant of adequate economic resources; in contrast, the court noted, the same was not stipulated in the new 2016 law, which stipulates a timeframe for development of such infrastructure. The court, in that landmark decision, outlined eleven directions that were significantly wide in scope, covering several aspects of accessibility. The scope of those directions included government buildings, airports, railways, government-owned transport carriers, as well as government websites. The guidelines also stipulated that the Bureau of Indian Standards embed the aspect of accessibility for the disabled in the National Building Code. This decision forms the bedrock for the decision of the Supreme Court in *Disabled Rights Group v. Union of India*, insofar as the adoption of the rights-based approach vis-à-vis accessibility is concerned.

4. *State of Himachal Pradesh v. Umed Ram Sharma*, (1986) 2 SCC 68

5. *Supra* note 3, para 12

The Supreme Court, while evaluating the definitions of 'establishment', 'government establishment', 'private establishment', 'public building', 'transportation systems', and 'universal designs' under the 2016 Act, noted that as per Sections 16(ii), 25(1)(b), and 40 of the 2016 Act, the 'appropriate government'[6] and the local authority was required, firstly, to endeavour that all funded and recognised educational institutions were dispensing inclusive education to Persons with Disabilities by making buildings and their campuses accessible to them. Secondly, as per the mandate of Section 25(1)(b), the appropriate government was to take necessary measures to ensure 'barrier-free access' to all government and private hospitals, and lastly, as per Section 40, the Central Government was to prescribe rules and lay out standards of accessibility for such institutions.

Additionally, the court noted that the aspect of accessibility to public buildings was also covered by the 'Harmonised Guidelines and Space Standards'.[7] In fact, the University Grants Commission (UGC) had also made provisions for 'schemes for Persons with Disabilities' such as the Higher Education for Persons with Special Needs, which outlined three main components. First, the establishment of enabling units for disabled persons; second, ensuring access to disabled persons by the introduction of a one-

---

6. Section 2(b), Persons with Disabilities Act, 2016, 'appropriate government' means –
(i) in relation to the Central Government or any establishment wholly or substantially financed by that government, or a Cantonment Board constituted under the Cantonments Act, 2006 (41 of 2006), the Central Government
(ii) in relation to a State Government or any establishment, wholly or substantially financed by that government, or any local authority, other than a Cantonment Board, the State Government

7. Representation of Persons with Disabilities (Amendment) Rules, 'Harmonised Guidelines and Space Standards for Universal Accessibility in India', Ministry of Housing and Urban Affairs, Government of India

time grant for colleges to enable an environment for mobility and independent functioning; and third, ensuring special equipment to augment educational services for disabled persons.

In view of the above, the Supreme Court held that every institution must ensure that its infrastructure, university/college campus, on-campus accommodation, classroom (for the visually impaired, orthopaedically impaired, and hearing impaired), science laboratories, libraries, pedagogy, mode of examinations and testing, recreational activities, and university administration are made accessible for disabled persons. The court directed the UGC to carry out an inspection to verify if the educational institutions are, in fact, 'disabled-friendly'. Notably, the Supreme Court also directed the UGC to form a Committee to evaluate the feasibility of implementing the petitioner's suggestions concerning the above aspects of accessibility while also stipulating a timeframe within which (by 30 June 2018) the entire exercise was to be carried out.

The above directions highlight how the Supreme Court, in the present decision, evaluated existing jurisprudence on the subject of accessibility to public institutions for disabled persons by recognising that these obstacles were socially constructed impediments presented before the disabled in myriad aspects of their education. Further, directions of the Supreme Court on the importance of structuring our pedagogical methods around the idea of accessibility are reflective of the Supreme Court's rights-based approach.

Understanding Accessibility with the Social Constructedness of Disability & Discrimination

While expatiating on the issue of making educational institutions more accessible for Persons with Disabilities, the judgment draws inspiration from capability theorists like Martha Nussbaum to highlight the importance that infrastructural accessibility holds for ensuring a level playing field for disabled persons. The judgment underscores how the absence of accessible infrastructure has the capacity to seriously impair the possibilities of a fruitful educational experience for disabled persons.

As a precursor to the judgment's eventual discussion of disability theory, the apex court interestingly notes, 'It hardly needs to be emphasised that Disabilities Act is premised on the fundamental idea that society creates the barriers and oppressive structures which impede the capacities of Persons with Disabilities.'[8] This neatly segues into the court's acknowledgment of lessons from the Social Model of Disability:

> ...The Social Model of Disability locates disability as being socially constructed through the creation of artificial attitudinal, organisational, and environmental barriers. Impairment is regarded as being a normal part of the human condition, with everyone experiencing impairment differently and having different access needs. Life is accepted as including negative experiences, and impairment may be – but is not necessarily – one of them. Disabled people are defined as being people who experience the unnecessary barriers created by society within their daily life. The Social Model of Disability has gained ground in the international debate. This views disability as a social construct and emphasises society's shortcomings, stigmatisation, and discrimination in its reaction to Persons with Disabilities. It distinguishes between functional impairments (disability), both of a physical and psychological nature, and the loss of equal participation in social processes that only arises through interaction with the

8. *Supra* note 1, para 15

> social setting (handicap). These developments have contributed to a new (WHO) model, which bears in mind social as well as functional and individual factors in its classification of health and health-related areas. Keeping in view the above, proper facilities need to be provided to disabled persons while having higher education.[9]

This acknowledgment of the social constructedness of handicaps resulting from disabilities is significant; it transforms the vantage point of viewing disability rights protection from that of social magnanimity to moral necessity. If one accepts that handicaps resulting from disabilities are largely a result of interaction with barriers constructed in social settings, then dislodging such socially constructed strictures becomes necessary as a matter of upholding the Dworkinian values of equal concern and equal respect that philosophically support democratic societies. The consequences of this realisation can be immensely empowering, not just for disabled persons but also for the societies they live and thrive in. In the same vein, the court writes:

> ...A disability is only actually a disability when it prevents someone from doing what they want or need to do. A lawyer can be just as effective in a wheelchair, as long as she has access to the courtroom and the legal library, as well as to whatever other places and materials or equipment that are necessary for her to do her job well. A person who can't hear can be a master carpenter or the head of a chemistry lab, if he can communicate with clients and assistants. A person with mental illness can nonetheless be a brilliant scholar or theorist.[10]

---

9. *Id.*, para 16

10. *Id.*, para 17

From this theoretical standpoint, a collective failure to displace strictures that limit disabled people's capacity for self-actualisation would amount to discrimination, and the Supreme Court recognises it as such in the context of making educational institutions more accessible:

> ...Not making adequate provisions to facilitate proper education to such persons, therefore, would amount to discrimination. Such requirement is to ensure that even a student with a disability, after proper education, will be able to lead an independent, economically self-sufficient, productive, and fully participatory life. This rights-based approach is an inclusive approach which calls for the participation of all groups of the population, including disadvantaged persons, in the development process. Inclusive development builds on the idea of 'Society for All' in which all people are equally free to develop their potential, contribute their skills and abilities for the common good, and take up their entitlements to social services. It emphasises strengthening the rights of people with disabilities and foster their participation in all aspects of life.[11]

Thus, it is clear from the court's analysis that it views accessibility as a rights-based imperative intricately yoked to lessons learnt from disability theory about the socially contingent nature of discrimination and disadvantages resulting from disabilities. As a first step, it is crucial to recognise the social constructedness of handicaps resulting from disabilities for the enablement of their eventual displacement. On that count, the court takes us towards a progressive jurisprudence of understanding accessibility in light of valuable insights from disability theory instead of relying on

11. *Ibid.*

outmoded notions of social benevolence. The court deserves plaudits for delivering to us a filigree of important directions aimed at bringing disabled persons closer to the constitutional promise of equality, a promise that remains a distant dream for disabled persons as a consequence of lives rife with obstacles. Against that backdrop, *Disabled Rights Group v. Union of India* opens a space for uncovering and dislodging structures that function in ableist ways.

◇◇

Jaideep Singh Lalli & Ananya Sharma

Jaideep Singh Lalli completed his BA LLB (Hons) with Distinction at Panjab University, Chandigarh. Throughout his qualifying law degree, he worked with advocates, human rights organisations, and judges of various courts. Motivated by his interest in comparative law and human rights, he worked with Senior Advocate Dr Menaka Guruswamy, Justice D.Y. Chandrachud (former Chief Justice of the Supreme Court of India) and Justice Sapana Pradhan Malla of the Supreme Court of Nepal.

In 2023, he completed his LLM from Trinity College, University of Cambridge, with a First-Class result. At Cambridge, Jaideep studied Criminal Justice and Human Rights Law, Legislation, Jurisprudence, and International Human Rights Law. He was awarded a Trinity College Exam Prize, the Lizette Bentwich Prize, and the title of Senior Scholar at Trinity for his excellent exam performance. He was further awarded the Cambridge Pro Bono Gold Award for his work on heading a research project on The

Gambia's gender-based violence law, completed for the Cambridge Pro Bono Project and the World Bank.

Additionally, he has written extensively on issues concerning discrimination law, criminal justice, organised crime, human rights, and land acquisition. His work has been published in the University of Oxford Human Rights Hub Journal, Statute Law Review (Oxford University Press), NALSAR (National Academy of Legal Studies and Research) Student Law Review, Journal of Victimology & Victim Justice, Kathmandu School of Law Review, among others. Jaideep's area of interest lies in discrimination law, criminal justice, constitutional law, family law, and strategic human rights litigation.

Ananya Sharma completed her BA LLB with Distinction at the Army Institute of Law, Mohali, Punjab, India. While pursuing law, she worked with many leading lawyers practicing in the Punjab and Haryana High Court. After graduating with a First-Class result, she pursued litigation primarily in disability and constitutional law, with additional experience in Intellectual Property Rights. Currently, she is working with an American company as an In-House Counsel, overseeing their Contracts Division and advising on other day-to-day legal affairs of the Company as well as its sister concerns. Beyond her current employment, Ananya's area of interest lies in disability law, constitutional law, and contract law.